IMMIGRATION AND ITS IMPACT ON AMERICAN CITIES

IMMIGRATION
AND ITS IMPACT ON
AMERICAN CITIES

Stephen C. Loveless,
Clifford P. McCue, Raymond B. Surette,
and Dorothy Norris-Tirrell

Westport, Connecticut
London

JV
6471
I44
1996

Library of Congress Cataloging-in-Publication Data

Immigration and its impact on American cities / Stephen C. Loveless
   . . . [et al.].
      p. cm.
   Includes bibliographical references and index.
   ISBN 0–275–94500–6 (alk. paper)
      1. United States—Emigration and immigration—Economic aspects.
2. Cities and towns—United States.   3. Municipal finance—United
States.   4. Municipal services—United States.   I. Loveless,
Stephen C.
JV6471.I44   1996
304.8'73—dc20   95–40580

British Library Cataloguing in Publication Data is available.

Library of Congress Catalog Card Number: 95–40580
ISBN: 0–275–94500–6

First published in 1996

Praeger Publishers, 88 Post Road West, Westport, CT 06881
An imprint of Greenwood Publishing Group, Inc.

Printed in the United States of America

The paper used in this book complies with the
Permanent Paper Standard issued by the National
Information Standards Organization (Z39.48–1984).

10 9 8 7 6 5 4 3 2 1

© 1982 Rayburn Beale

IN MEMORY OF
STEPHEN CRAWFORD LOVELESS
1950–1992

This book is dedicated to the memory of Stephen C. Loveless. Although he died before the project came to fruition, Steve was instrumental in its creation. The completion of this book by two of Steve's students demonstrates his impact as a scholar and professor. After knowing Steve for twenty-five years, I came to respect his high intellectual energy and commitment to the advancement of the field of Public Administration. This book honors Steve both as an academician and as a dedicated father, friend, student, and colleague. We will all miss the compassion and enthusiasm he showed in his life and his work.

James D. Carroll
Florida International University

Contents

Illustrations

FIGURES

Preface

This book is about how immigration affects American cities and how local government decision makers can effectively manage immigration's impacts. In 1990, an estimated 1.5 million legal immigrants entered the United States. While immigration policy is the purview of the federal government, cities, as host communities, bear a substantial financial burden for the direct provision of services utilized by immigrants. Previous empirical research on immigration focuses largely on federal and state impacts, neglecting local-level impacts. As a result, local governments have not developed the strategies necessary for evaluating the specific effects of immigration for purposes of decision making and planning. In addition, local officials have not effectively lobbied for increased resources from state and federal channels. Therefore, this book addresses the following fundamental question: What impacts do immigrants have on local government revenues and expenditures?

This question is particularly important because the number of immigrants and their magnitude of effect on government is expected to grow (General Accounting Office, 1994). The migration process creates its own self-propelling momentum as early immigrants attract fellow countrymen (Massey, 1990). In addition, recent revisions of immigration law have substantially expanded the number of annual visas. Agreements with Cuba, and instability in Eastern Europe, the former Soviet Union, the Far East, and various Caribbean and Latin American nations suggest that the flow of immigration may accelerate exponentially over the next two decades.

The effects of contemporary immigration patterns are compounded because the current wave is suggested to be very different from past waves. Rather than a concentration from a few European countries, immigrants today come from virtually every region of the world, expanding the variety of languages and cultural norms that must be accommodated, as well as the demands placed on government services.

Faced with a likely future of continued or expanding migration to the United States, this book argues that only a concentrated, multistrategy approach will provide needed information for local government decision makers facing immigration. The book has three purposes. First, the book expands the current literature examining impacts of immigration. As noted, the bulk of existing research on immigration focuses on benefits and costs to federal- and state-level governments. However, cities, as host communities to incoming immigrants, are the providers of basic services and, therefore, may be more directly impacted. Findings from a case study focusing on the City of Miami, Florida, suggest that past immigration is associated with increases in both expenditures and revenues. However, expenditures exceed revenues over the study period (including direct federal and state support), particularly in the early years of an immigrant's arrival.

The second purpose of the book is to introduce an impact model as an analytical tool for determining immigration effects. The model is provided as a technical device useful to local government decision makers. Often, decision makers intuitively understand that existing problems are direct consequences of immigration. The model offers a method for empirical investigation of immigrant impacts across services and revenue sources. The model utilizes multiple methods for collecting and interpreting quantitative and qualitative data, and allows for consideration of both large-scale idiosyncratic flows and stable annual immigration.

The book's third purpose is to assist local government decision makers in planning, managing, and, to some degree, controlling immigration in a given jurisdiction. The book uses the City of Miami, Florida, as a case study for illustrating the model and its utility for decision making. The inclusion of a case study allows the impact of immigration to be scrutinized from a practical perspective.

OVERVIEW OF THE CONTENTS

Chapter 1 sets the context for examining the fiscal impacts of immigration on local governments through a brief historical overview of immigration as it is related to municipal development. Based on the findings from the existing literature, four assumptions are presented to establish the foundation for the introduction of a seven-step model. The model is the first integrated attempt to extrapolate immigrant impacts using both quantitative and qualitative methods. The case study setting is also described.

Chapter 2 focuses on the methods for enumerating immigrants in a particular community. After a discussion of the commonly used terminology related to immigration, various concerns when estimating documented and undocumented immigrants are discussed. Methods for addressing the inadequacies are presented.

Chapter 3 moves to the collection of primary data about immigrants through the use of a field survey. The survey allows decision makers to examine the immigrants in a given community through questions focused on demographics, decision making processes, and attitudes toward government. Of particular interest are the following questions: Why did they decide to immigrate? What information and sources of information were utilized in their decision to immigrate? What criteria did they use in determining where to reside in the United States upon immigration? What services were they most likely to utilize when they arrived?

Chapter 4 gathers expert perspective through the use of a Delphi survey. National and local experts are questioned for their predictions of the numbers and characteristics of future immigrants and the resulting impacts on local governments.

Chapter 5 combines annual revenue and expenditure data with the immigration estimates developed in Chapter 2 to generate a baseline of associated fiscal impacts. A series of hypotheses delineated by service area (i.e., police, fire, emergency medical, sanitation, public works, and personnel management) are used as a tool to assist decision makers in sensitizing the data analysis to their particular jurisdictions.

Forecasting is the subject of Chapter 6, as predictions of future documented and undocumented immigration are developed. The forecasting methods incorporate findings from previous chapters to produce a range of estimates.

Chapter 7 synthesizes all of the quantitative and qualitative data to project the impact of immigration on local government revenues and expenditures. In addition, conclusions are offered about the model as well as the nonfiscal effects of immigration on American cities.

The appendixes serve as resources to municipal decision makers in implementing the steps of the model, by providing copies of the field survey and Delphi surveys discussed in the text.

This book bridges the gap between research findings and techniques to help cope with overall immigration for local government managers. Municipal officials need baseline information and techniques for analyzing data to improve responsiveness to immigrants and for pursuing and justifying financial support from state and federal levels of government. The information and resources presented here should provide guidance to municipal decision makers in managing the multiple impacts of immigration on their communities.

ACKNOWLEDGMENTS

This book began as a research grant from the State of Florida Institute of Government to develop methods for forecasting the impact of immigration on the provision of municipal services. With Stephen C. Loveless as the principal investigator, the research team was composed of faculty and graduate students who were then at Florida International University, School of Public Affairs and Services. Other than the authors, the team members were Dolores Brosnan, Clinton Terry, Lidia Tuttle, and Bernice Matalon.

CHAPTER 1_____

Examining the
Impact of Immigration
on City Government

Immigration policy and its implementation have played a vital role in the economic, demographic, political, and social evolution of the United States. Since the country's inception, media headlines and political debate have cried for immigration reform, specifically regarding the quantity and country of origin of entering immigrants. In recent years, population movements into and out of the United States have attracted increased scrutiny because immigration is reportedly linked to many social and economic problems.

Primary to the current debate regarding immigration policy is determining the impact that immigrants have on public services. Supporters of "closed-door" policies argue that immigrants take jobs away from current citizens and consume too many public services, yet do not contribute their fair share of tax dollars in support of public programs. Consequently, immigrants cost society in terms of human capital, economic resources, and public programs. Closed-door advocates, therefore, desire to limit the flow of immigrants entering the United States. Proponents of "open-door" policies counter that immigrants have been the backbone of economic growth throughout U.S. history because they tend to assume menial tasks that indigenous Americans avoid. They contend that barring these individuals from immigrating potentially limits the growth of the economy, as well as severely hampers the social and cultural transition of the United States. Further, open-door advocates stress that immigrants quickly become productive, taxpaying members of the community and do not unfairly burden current citizens or use proportionately higher levels of public services than their native counterparts.

Past research examining the fiscal impacts of immigration on public services focuses largely on federal and state programs. However, local governments provide the bulk of services to immigrants and, therefore, bear the brunt of immigration costs (Simon, 1982; Muller and Espenshade, 1985; Collins, 1991; Bogen, 1987). As the role of local governments in service provision has expanded over the twentieth century, so has their financial obligation for those services. Currently, local governments have varying responsibilities for demand-responsive programs such as education, health, and social welfare services, areas traditionally seen as strongly affected by immigration (General Accounting Office, 1994). Local governments also provide direct services, such as police, parks, and sanitation, that are often overlooked when studying immigrant impacts on public expenditures.

A compounding factor facing local government decision makers is their lack of control over the number of immigrants settling within their jurisdiction (Basch, 1983). The reasons for immigration to the United States (primarily political, economic, or family reunification) are virtually immune to municipal manipulation. Moreover, where immigrants reside once in the United States depends much more on the location of fellow countrymen and family than on any policy attempting to deter such enclave development.

Complicating an examination of the impacts of immigration on local governments is the fact that the costs for providing services to immigrants are not shared equally among municipalities. A disproportionate number of arriving immigrants locate in particular cities. However, as the immigrants become established, both economically and socially, they move from the original "host" city to other, more prosperous communities and are replaced by a new set of arriving immigrants. Therefore, the jurisdictions which act as host communities finance the initial socialization and conditioning costs, without the benefit of increasing revenues and community development as the immigrants become more economically established.

Public officials, policy analysts, and academicians agree that immigration has substantial consequences for local government revenue and expenditure considerations (Clark, 1994; Heer, 1990; Simon, 1981). Prior research efforts analyzing the effects of immigration on municipalities suggest that immigrant populations generate net benefits and costs to local governments. However, little systematic research has examined the fiscal impact of legal and undocumented immigrants on American cities (General Accounting Office, 1994; Rothman and Espenshade, 1992). Local government decision makers, therefore, lack analytical tools for analyzing immigration impacts.

This chapter introduces a model for determining the effects of immigration on local governments. The model is designed to provide municipal decision makers with the tools and theoretical framework for analyzing immigration's impact on their respective communities. Following a short historical overview of immigration and city governance, previous research is presented pertaining to a key area of the debate regarding immigration—determining the fiscal impacts of immigration on local government. The seven-step model upon which the book is based is then briefly introduced.

IMMIGRATION AND CITY GOVERNMENT: A HISTORICAL PERSPECTIVE

A primary assumption of immigration studies is that past immigration patterns are a prologue to current and future immigration. Therefore, a brief historical review of immigration and municipal administration provides a foundation for studying contemporary relationships. While the growth and transition of American cities is not thought to solely reflect the influence of immigration, a historical review does demonstrate the concurrent nature of city development and immigration s role in developing and expanding the nation.

After the first English and Puritan immigrants established initial colonial cities at Jamestown in 1607, and Plymouth in 1620, subsequent immigration to the United States is best described as "welcome tinged with misgiving" (Jones, 1960, p. 40). The desire for greater economic opportunity, freedom from political oppression and persecution, and religious freedom initiated the first wave of migration from Europe during the 1600s and the birth of America's cities (U.S. Immigration and Naturalization Service, 1987). To many emerging colonies, newly arriving immigrants provided practical benefits, such as cheap labor for harvesting fertile soils, a means of promoting land settlements and expanding frontiers, and a source of additional revenues for colonial governments and merchants. Not all immigrants were viewed with the same enthusiasm, however. To limit the flow of "undesirables," port colonies such as New York and Boston implemented head taxes on vessels which brought passengers from Ireland, Germany, and France. In addition, many colonial governments required vessel captains to post bond to insure that their passengers would not become public charges.

As a result, immigration during the seventeenth century was minimal. However, the early eighteenth century marked a period of relatively high migration to the United States, with newly arriving immigrants coming primarily from non-English-speaking countries. During this period, individuals of non-English decent migrated in such large numbers "as to alter markedly the ethnic composition of nearly every colony" (Jones, 1960, p. 22). From America's earliest settlements, the government, religion, and social class structure displayed amazing diversity. Colonies, such as Massachusetts and New York, were organized around religious lines. Others, like Maryland and Virginia, were feudal in nature, prescribing certain privileges for property owners. Still others were more democratic, like Rhode Island and Pennsylvania, which granted all "freemen" a voice in colonial government

as well as the right to religious worship without fear of persecution or re-
jection (Wright, 1971).

Consistent with the diverse development of the colonies was the growth
of equally diverse American cities. Prior to the arrival of various non-English immigrant groups, colonial cities were primarily distinguished by ter-
rain, climate, and natural resources. As "new" immigrants arrived and their
numbers increased, ethnically based social and culture factors played more
important roles in colonial development.

Expanding the Nation: 1790–1860

At the time of the first official federal census in 1790, the population of
the Unite States was approximately 3.2 million. More than 75 percent of the
nation's inhabitants were of British descent, while 8 percent were German
and the remainder either Spanish, French, Irish, or Dutch (U.S. Select
Commission on Immigration and Refugee Policy, 1981). Although American Indians and Blacks were not enumerated in this family portrait, approximately 350,000 to 500,000 black slaves and an equal amount of
American Indians inhabited the United States at this time (Jones, 1960;
Chickering, 1848).

In 1790, Congress passed the first naturalization statute, which defined
who would be eligible for citizenship. In addition to prescribing citizenship,
many politicians felt that more stringent congressional action was necessary
to effectively control immigration. Thus, in 1798, Congress created the
Alien Enemies Act and the Alien Friends Act, which gave the president the
power to expel any immigrant considered a threat to the well-being of the
nation. Enforcement of these politically abused acts soon waned and they
were allowed to expire in 1800 (U.S. Immigration and Naturalization Service, 1991). However, the precedent for immigration policies being set at
the federal level was established.

Legislation passed in 1802, 1812, and 1819, formalized processes of citizenship, immigration, and deportation. In particular, an act passed in 1802
required the following for citizenship: a five-year residency, denouncement
of previous political affiliations, surrendering titles of nobility, good moral
character, and posting a formal declaration of intent to uphold the Consti-
tution (U.S. Immigration and Naturalization Service, 1991).

Although pre–Revolutionary War immigration established the foundation for colonial growth, it was no match for the mass migration of the nineteenth century. Over the "Century of Immigration," roughly 20 million
people, drawn from every corner of Europe, made their way to America.
During this post-Revolutionary period, American city governments began
to transform from "closed corporations," developed under British rule, to
popularly elected city councils more compatible with democratic ideals.
Among cities established under British influence during colonial times,

public officials were normally appointed for life and, in most cases, would select their successor. However, this form of governance did not fare well with republican ideologies of separation of powers and checks and balances. It was not long after the Revolution that democratic forms of governance appeared in most American cities.

In 1796 and 1797, the states of Philadelphia and Maryland required all new city charters to establish bicameral city councils. Detroit, Boston, and New York soon followed suit. Participation in these councils was limited by the citizenship legislation of the period. Furthermore, none of the major cities provided consistent public assistance programs to immigrants in acquiring housing, work, or locating relatives. Hence, while immigration was shaping the social and economic life of cities, immigrants were not fully involved in, or beneficiaries of, municipal political life during this period.

The Industrial Period: 1860–1920

With the end of the Civil War and the stabilization of the economy, migration to the United States again soared. As a result of the devastation caused by the Civil War and the increased use of production machinery in industry, American merchants experienced a sharp need for industrial workers. This prompted Congress to pass the Act to Encourage Immigration in 1864, which allowed U.S. employers to actively recruit foreign workers.[1]

Throughout the latter nineteenth century, the introduction of machinery and other forms of technology greatly altered the quantity and characteristics of migration to the United States and, concurrently, municipal development. Between 1850 and 1920, the population of American cities grew by an astonishing 700 percent. Not only were rural Americans moving to the cities to seek employment in manufacturing industries, but immigrants were flooding into U.S. cities and forming the foundation of U.S. urbanization.

By 1910, roughly 40 percent of city inhabitants were immigrants. A pattern of municipal development was emerging whereby new immigrant groups would arrive and settle into pre-existing ethnic neighborhoods, while older, more economically established immigrants would move elsewhere, typically to outlying suburban neighborhoods. Further, most of these newer immigrants entered the United States as poor rural farmers, and city life was typically fashioned along lines of nationality. Consequently, core urban areas began to transform into "enclave mosaics" (Glaab, 1967, p. 139). However, the development of enclave cities (both politically and economically) did not bode well with native sentiment. As a result, many citizens felt that the new immigrants, predominantly Roman Catholic and Jewish, were very much different from the old.

Immigrant enclaves, coupled with the growth of many American suburbs, required administrative and institutional change. Prior to the urbanization of the United States, many of the services provided to immigrants came in the form of volunteer organizations or private immigrant associations. A series of makeshift political and administrative responses met the demands of urbanization and the growing distrust of the newest immigrants. The boss–machine form of governance grew as a means for immigrants to express political influence and secure employment. Labor unions began to emerge and voice immigrant based dissatisfaction with employment conditions and pay. Basic municipal services were increasingly demanded as a result of poor sanitation and living conditions among immigrants and requests by Americans for increased police protection due to growing urban crime and violence.

Out of the apparent chaos and necessity, city governments were also becoming more involved in the development and administration of public programs. The first major area of local government expansion was in education, followed by public health, housing reform, police and fire, and public parks. Accompanying the growth in municipal government services were increases in local tax burdens.

In response to rampant political corruption and an ever-increasing tax burden from growing public programs, a national call for local government reform was sparked. Although the reform of local governments varied widely from state to state, certain key elements of the movement emerged, including a steady movement away from state interference in local government affairs through "home rule" amendments. In addition, executive authority at the local level was promoted. The hope was that public programs would be streamlined and simplified by means of economy and expert management.

Between the Wars: 1920–1954

In the aftermath of World War I, immigration to the United States began anew. By 1920, immigration had expanded by 300 percent over 1919. However, the "Red Scare," depressing economic conditions, and increased demands for adequate housing witnessed during the 1930s prompted Congress to numerically limit certain groups of individuals from migrating into this country. With the passage of the Immigration and Naturalization Act of 1924, the first official quota system of the United States was established. Although the intention of the 1924 act was to numerically limit individuals from "undesirable" nations, a consequence of the act was the first wave of illegal immigration. Immigrants from the "barred" zones (e.g., most Asiatic countries) and Europe who did not qualify for legal immigration typically migrated to Canada and Mexico, nations not subject to quota restraints, and then entered the United States through unofficial channels. By the early 1930s, a whole industry of smuggling aliens had arisen as an unforeseen consequence of the 1924 act. However, the Depression dampened the economic lure of the United States and suppressed immigration to minimal levels.

After World War I and recovery from the Depression of the 1930s, local governments were no longer the focus of administrative reform and policy formation. The federal government and, as a secondary effect, state governments, became primary service providers. In fact, since many of the public service programs were federally funded and directed, local governments stagnated and lost political influence both with the states and with Washington during this period. The extensive centralization of policy and power resulted in the general acceptance of imposed policies from external sources at the local level. Immigration policy was no exception.

Contemporary Immigration: 1954–Present

In the aftermath of World War II, immigration to the United States reached new heights. Between 1961 and 1990, some 15.4 million immigrants made their way to this country. These "new" immigrants were predominately from Mexico and the Caribbean (33 percent of the total immigrants admitted), while Asians represented around 16 percent of the immigrant population growth.

The 1952 Immigration and Nationality Act (the McCarran–Walter Act) introduced registration of intent in the country of origin prior to visa issuance, and required noncitizens currently residing in the United States to file annual address forms with the U.S. Immigration and Naturalization Service (INS) or face deportation. With legislation that followed in 1965, immigrant visas were distributed according to a seven-category preference system, placing priority on attracting needed skills, family reunification, and assisting political refugees.

During the 1970s and early 1980s, additional amendments completed the transition from the largely quota-based system to the legal criteria-based immigration system which is currently in place. The most recent major legislation, the Immigration Reform and Control Act (IRCA) of 1986, granted illegal aliens residing in the United States an opportunity to officially change their residency status. This legislation, although heralded as a "humanitarian" effort, was primarily passed as a means of dealing with the growing illegal alien population residing in the United States.

One of the most striking results of contemporary trends in immigration is that in 1990, nearly 8 percent of the total U.S. population was foreign born. Further, one in four of the estimated 20 million foreign-born residents entered the country between 1985 and 1990, and roughly 60 percent of these individuals were not citizens in 1990 (U.S. Bureau of the Census, 1993).

National immigration totals, however, do not account for the tendency of immigrants to reside in certain states and locate within certain communities. For example, roughly 44 percent of all immigrants to the United States in 1990 selected California as their primary state of residency (Table 1.1). Moreover, about 55 percent of those immigrants residing in California live in Los Angeles County. An additional phenomena is the continuing and dominant tendency of ethnic enclaves to form, such as the large Mexican population residing in Los Angeles County. Of the 374,773 immigrants living

Table 1.1
Immigrants* Admitted, by Intended Residence (State) and Country of Birth
(Year Ending September 30, 1990)

	Total	Europe	Asia	North America	South America	Africa
Total	1,536,483	112,401	338,581	957,558	85,819	35,893
California	682,979	21,417	130,814	510,106	12,105	5,344
New York	189,589	26,392	45,628	78,610	31,251	7,424
Texas	174,132	2,828	16,805	148,302	2,837	3,162
Illinois	83,858	12,358	14,549	53,472	2,188	1,223
Florida	71,603	6,021	8,122	13,395	12,827	1,114
New Jersey	52,670	8,016	15,808	14,760	11,354	2,670
Massachusetts	25,338	6,118	8,273	7,640	1,487	1,747
Arizona	23,737	866	2,797	19,528	257	209
Virginia	19,000	1,500	9,400	4,500	1,600	1,500

Source: U.S. Immigration and Naturalization Service, *Statistical Yearbook, 1990* (Washington, D.C.: U.S. Government Printing Office, 1991).
*For definition of immigrants, see text, Chapter 2.

in Los Angeles in 1990, 62 percent were Mexican, while the next highest
immigrant population of Los Angeles was El Salvadorian, representing
about 11 percent of the total immigrant population.

The demographic composition and cultural norms present in most cities are
a product of immigration or migration. The historical waves of immigration
have directly influenced the growth and transition of cities in the United
States and will continue to be the focus of debate as local government decision makers struggle with the fiscal and social impacts of immigration.

RESEARCH EXAMINING THE
FISCAL IMPACT OF IMMIGRATION

As highlighted in the previous section, many legislative attempts to stave the
flow of immigration were predicated on the assumption that immigrants
negatively impact society. However, most of these policy efforts were based
on beliefs and speculations, rather than substantive policy analysis. Empirical research examining the impacts of immigration on the nation did not
begin to emerge until the mid-1970s.

Previous research emphasizes federal and state service provision at the
expense of the more dynamic impacts of immigration on local governments.
Contrary to public opinion, prior studies have determined that, in general,
immigrants pay more in tax revenues to federal and state governments than
they use in public services. Therefore, a primary question in examining the
impact of immigrants on cities is this: Do immigrants pay more local taxes
and fees in support of local government services than they consume?

To assist local government decision makers in considering this question, the research presented here is guided by four assumptions that imply immigrants, in general, have positive net economic impact, but that these benefits do not occur to municipalities. The propositions presented below integrate the observations and findings in the literature regarding immigrant impacts on host communities.[2] Although the assumptions discussed are necessary to develop an understanding of the financial impacts of immigration on the receiving community, they may not sufficiently explain idiosyncratic impacts at different levels of government or across specific revenue or expenditure items.

In developing these assumptions, differences in phrasing, logic, and research focus expressed by the reviewed authors have, of necessity, been smoothed out. Nevertheless, the assumptions provide a reasonable summary of the major points of consensus in the literature, and are further augmented by the recent review of impact research conducted by Rothman and Espenshade (1992), and the findings of Clark (1994) and the General Accounting Office (1994).

Assumption 1: Newly arriving legal and illegal immigrants are less likely to participate in public assistance programs than their indigenous counterparts. Many scholars suggest that when immigrants first arrive in the United States they are unfamiliar with, or are reluctant to participate in, public programs available to address their particular needs (Simon, 1981, 1984; Tienda and Jensen, 1986; Borjas and Trejo, 1991; Blau, 1984). Therefore, newly arriving immigrants contribute more in taxes (federal and/or state income taxes and sales taxes) than they consume in public services (e.g., Aid for Families with Dependent Children [AFDC], Medicare, and food stamps). As a result, immigrants provide a net financial benefit for federal and state governments.

On the federal level, this point is more obvious than on the state level. As Heer (1990) uncovered, both undocumented and legal immigrants participated less than native citizens in many public assistance programs offered by the federal government, and contributed roughly equivalent payments in the form of federal income taxes.[3]

Research by Borjas and Trejo (1991) and Tienda and Jensen (1986) report similar findings and confirm that legal immigrants are considerably less likely to become welfare participants than natives. In sum, past research demonstrates, although not conclusively, that utilization rates for public assistance programs are higher for Americans than for immigrants, when other demographic determinants such as age, gender, education, and marital status are held constant. This suggests that federal policy toward immigration may be liberal because the fiscal burden of providing services to immigrants is shifted to other levels of government (Rothman and Espenshade, 1992).

Another factor potentially limiting the financial impact on the federal level is that illegal aliens are not eligible for many demand-responsive services, such as Supplemental Security Income (SSI), food stamps, AFDC, or

unemployment compensation. Illegal aliens are eligible, however, to partici-
pate in certain programs, such as Head Start or the Special Supplemental
Food Stamp Program for Women, Infants, and Children (General Accounting
Office, 1994).

Immigrant impact on the state level is not as clearly delineated, and local-level impacts are even more problematic. One of the reasons cited for
the disparity is that the federal government has "bumping rights" (Rothman
and Espenshade, 1992). Thus, the federal government has, and often uses,
the authority to require specific immigration and refugee programs by state
and local governments. Concurrently, the federal government can shift the
financial burden of providing these mandated services to other levels of
government, while retaining the financial benefit of revenue from income
taxes.[4]

Further complicating the cost and benefits assessment quagmire is that
state governments also employ the same bumping privileges. The end result
is that the local level of government is saddled with most of the financial
burden of providing direct services to immigrants, while not receiving the
total tax benefits that immigrants provide (Simon, 1981).

*Assumption 2: The propensity of immigrants to use public assistance pro-
grams increases as their time of residency in the United States increases. However, the amount of taxes paid by immigrants increases at a rate faster than
service utilization on the federal and state level.*

Many researchers have demonstrated that as immigrants become more
familiar with available public services, they have a higher propensity to participate in these programs (North and Houston, 1976; Simon, 1984). However, as participation rates increase, so does the earning capacity of
immigrants. Thus, the net effect of an increased utilization rate is offset by
an increase in wages earned and taxes paid. In addition, other researchers
have determined that over the time horizon of immigrants' stays, they remain less likely to receive assistance than citizens and contribute more in
taxes than they use in public programs.

Simon's (1981, 1984, 1985) work provides a cohort analysis of all foreign-
born U.S. residents categorized by year of entry, using the U.S. Census
Bureau's 1976 Survey of Income and Education (SIE). This analysis determined that immigrant families who had arrived after 1964 used substantially less in federal programs, such as SSI, AFDC, food stamps, and public
housing, than immigrant families who arrived between 1950 and 1964. The
research of Heer (1990), North and Houston (1976), and Tienda and Jensen
(1986) reached similar conclusions.

More recently, contradictory findings are provided by Borjas and Trejo
(1991) in their analysis of length of stay and its effects on utilization rates of
public services by immigrants.[5] Their study uses data from both the 1970
and 1980 censuses of population. Borjas and Trejo observed intracohort
changes in welfare participation rates between the two census periods and

determined that likelihood of participation in welfare programs for immigrants grew faster than citizen participation rates over the time horizon of the study.

In addition, researchers have differentiated immigrants by country of origin to determine if there are relationships between demographic characteristics of immigrants and rates of welfare participation. In all, the research suggests that immigrants from European, Asian, and African countries are less likely to participate in welfare programs than immigrants from the Western Hemisphere. In conclusion, the findings in support of this assumption are mixed and appear to be dependent upon the immigrant group under consideration.

Assumption 3. It is uncertain whether undocumented aliens pose a fiscal burden or benefit to governments, specifically at the state and local level.

Despite an intense and long-standing interest in the impact of illegal immigration on government services, the fiscal effects of undocumented immigrants remain open to debate. One of the most intensive studies examining the effects of illegal immigrants on state and local government services was conducted by Muller and Espenshade (1985). These researchers analyzed the economic consequences of undocumented and documented Mexican immigrants in California. Combining data from the 1980 census, various state and local government financial documents, and school district reports, the researchers compared California's revenues and expenditures (for both the State of California and Los Angeles County) using Mexican heads of households as their primary unit of analysis.

Examining the revenue side of the fiscal equation, Muller and Espenshade determined that, during the study period, the average Mexican immigrant generated $1,425 in tax revenues while the state spent roughly $3,204 on services (e.g., education, public welfare, healthcare, and highways). The net effect of Mexican migrants on the California and Los Angeles County governments was that each immigrant in the study produced a net fiscal burden of $1,779 to the state and $140 to the county for fiscal year 1980.

In contrast, Weintraub and Cardenas (1984) examined the effects of undocumented aliens on Texas state revenues and expenditures. These researchers gathered data from interviews with undocumented aliens and from program service providers having large numbers of undocumented aliens as clients, to estimate public service use and work habits. Through extensive interviews and data analysis, the researchers concluded that, in 1982, the average undocumented alien in Texas provided a net fiscal benefit to the state of between $195 and $214.

Variation across these and other research findings can be attributed not only to methodological differences, but to the methods employed to enumerate undocumented aliens residing in a particular jurisdiction (General Accounting Office, 1994). Since Muller and Espenshade's analysis did not segregate many local services utilized by individuals or attempt to determine what portion of Mexican immigrants were undocumented, their California impact conclusions may be more relevant for legal immigrants.

Further, since a large portion of Los Angeles County's own source revenues consists of property taxes and user charges, failure to account for these revenues may artificially underestimate the positive economic impact on the county. Furthermore, the level and cost of services provided by California and Texas differ in important ways that are likely to influence the fiscal impact on each state. Although the California analysis provides a possible correlation between service consumption and revenue production of Mexican heads of households, it is not definitive in concluding that the overall effect of undocumented aliens on either revenue or expenditure considerations at the local level is positive.

On the other hand, the Weintraub and Cardenas Texas-based analysis provides useful information about the effects of illegal immigrants on the local economy. However, their work is also subject to some of the same constraints as the Muller and Espenshade analysis, in that there was no attempt to isolate and evaluate the effects of illegal aliens on local-source revenues. This may be because it is easier to separate those revenue items that are collected on a state basis, like sales tax revenues or other intergovernment revenues, rather than the individual nature of local-source revenues.

A second limitation to the Texas study is that there was no longitudinal analysis completed on this population. If undocumented aliens behave similarly to documented immigrants in public services utilization rates and revenue-generating ability, it might be argued that, over time, their impacts would be similar to documented aliens or natives. However, there is no empirical evidence available suggesting similarities or differences. If the behavior of the undocumented population differs from that of a legal immigrant population, there is the need to examine the effects of illegal aliens over time and across revenue and expenditures separately. This is particularly important at the local level.

A major problem in comparing the results of previous research is the divergent nature of data and methods used for sampling undocumented aliens. Data collection techniques include interviews with legal and illegal immigrants and service providers, surveys of agencies which provide assistance to undocumented immigrants, and analysis of secondary census and INS data. The analysis of impacts also utilizes a range of methods for developing immigrant profiles, surveying providers, assessing the service utilization rate between citizens and immigrants, and extrapolating census figures to estimate immigrant populations. None of the methods employed have provided consistent findings (Rothman and Espenshade, 1992; General Accounting Office, 1994).

Due to the inconsistent findings of local-level research, Rothman and Espenshade suggest that future research should examine the impact of both legal and illegal aliens by integrating the demographic, economic, and behavioral characteristics of immigrants and comparing these to citizens.[6] Although this research effort commenced prior to the suggestions of Rothman and Espenshade, it does capture differences between various immigrant populations and emphasizes a triangulation of methods for data collection and analysis.

Assumption 4: Local governments provide the most direct public assistance programs to both legal and illegal immigrants, yet receive only a minor portion of public revenues generated from this population.

While research has generally concluded that immigrants provide a net fiscal benefit to governments, when these studies are desegregated by level of government, a consistent theme emerges. Fiscal benefits of immigration appear most frequently at the federal and state level, while fiscal costs are more prone to appear at the local level. This is partly due to the combined effects of the previously cited bumping privileges, and partly to the fact that local governments provide the most direct services to immigrant populations.

Weintraub and Cardenas (1984, p. 88) conclude that it is almost certain that undocumented persons contribute more to the revenue of the State of Texas than it costs the state to provide services. The opposite is true for local governments. The services provided on the local level are those most heavily utilized by undocumented aliens, but revenues contributed by these individuals go primarily to the state and federal governments. Therefore, state and federal governments realize a net fiscal benefit from revenues attributable to illegal aliens, while local governments bear an unfair financial burden.

Another reason for the negative local impact is the nature of government goods provided at various levels. Local governments provide the most direct programs to immigrants. Federal services, on the other hand, include many "public goods," such as defense, environmental protection, and international commerce, that are typically not analyzed in fiscal-impact studies. Further, state governments often act as a fiscal pass-through to local governments in such service areas as education, health, and welfare.

Even when public-goods expenditures are taken into account, local governments are providing a majority of services to both legal and illegal immigrants. Therefore, when the intergovernment components of service provision are held constant, the overall effect is for costs to accumulate at the local level. From this review, it was determined that local governments provide the bulk of public services to immigrants without access to the enhanced revenues generated by this population (Simon, 1981).

A MODEL FOR DETERMINING IMMIGRATION IMPACTS

Guided by these four assumptions, the techniques developed herein will provide city managers and policy makers with methods to evaluate impacts in their respective communities. As Figure 1.1 illustrates, the impact model consists of seven steps. Independently, each step generates useful information, but when all steps of the model are utilized, the final product provides tools for planning, managing, and, to a modest degree, controlling immigration impacts in communities. The steps are briefly described in the following sections and discussed further in a chapter dedicated to each topic.

Step 1: Documenting the Immigrant Population

The first step is enumerating immigrants residing in the jurisdiction of interest. This necessitates gathering official figures from various federal sources and adjusting these estimates with local indicators to obtain a relatively unbiased measure of immigration. To properly explain impacts, practical and reliable data should be collected historically. These data provide the baseline information for subsequent steps. They should include direct measures of legal immigrants and estimates of undocumented immigrants.

Step 2: Anticipating Immigrant Plans: A Field Survey

This step requires gathering information about immigrant plans. The field survey is a practical and inexpensive technique for capturing immigrant perceptions, and should focus on two primary decisions made by all immigrants: the decision to immigrate and the decision where to reside in the United States. The field interviews provide a means of gathering information that is often missing from official data, and allows local government officials

Figure 1.1
Model for Extrapolating Immigrant Impacts

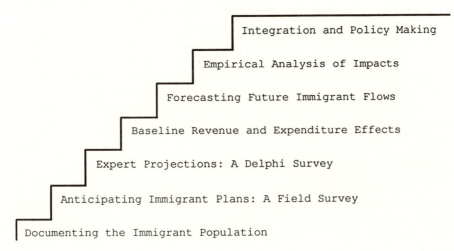

to check their own assumptions regarding the attitudes, perceptions, and plans of incoming immigrants.

Step 3: Expert Projections: A Delphi Survey

The collection and analysis of expert estimates of future immigration and its impact (using a Delphi survey technique) is employed as the third step in the model. A combination Delphi–cross-impact analysis technique is used to gather expert opinion concerning future immigration trends and the impacts of immigration on municipal services. While a steady flow of immigrants can be predicted with reasonable accuracy based on past immigration trends in addition to current quota limitations, major "events" such as the Mariel Boat Lift or Haitian Revolution radically alter the number of immigrants and mix of nationalities within a short time span. These shifts cannot be predicted by standard statistical forecasting techniques. Similarly, there may be immigration effects on service provision and interactions which cannot be discerned statistically. Structured expert opinion is employed to address both issues.

Step 4: Generation of Baseline Revenue and Expenditure Effects

This step begins with the collection of archival data on revenues and expenditures by local government functions (i.e., police, fire, emergency medical, sanitation, public works, and personnel management). By combining these data with INS- and census-based data regarding immigration numbers, the current relationship between revenue and expenditures and immigration is examined and a baseline for determining economic impacts is provided.

The statistical method for analyzing impacts is an autoregressive moving average method (ARIMA). Although the technique may seem ominous, it is relatively easy to understand and apply. One of the primary reasons for utilizing this approach is that the lagged effect of immigration on municipal revenues and expenditures must be considered. The source technique employed is a distributed lag regression analysis (Pindyck and Rubinfeld, 1981). The technique yields estimates of the initial impact of aggregate immigration by various nationalities during a given year t and the impact of year t immigration on services in subsequent years.

Step 5: Forecasting Future Immigration Flows

Next, a quantitative forecast of future immigration and the dispersion of immigrants between and among governments is developed. Using the baseline immigration numbers and the expert predictions from the Delphi, a range of projections is developed.

Step 6: Empirical Analysis of Impacts

The model of past effects and the estimation of future immigration are used in conjunction with the results of the Delphi and the field survey to construct a forecast of immigration impacts over the next decade. Since the projection of future numbers and changes in impact are based on estimates, a set of alternative outcomes is generated with their associated probabilities of occurrence.

Step 7: Integration and Policy Making

The final step of the model, and perhaps the most difficult, is integrating the findings of the previous six steps in a manner that policy makers can utilize to plan, manage, and to a marginal extent, control immigration effects. Although the individual steps can provide fruitful information to better understand the impacts of immigration on local revenues and expenditures, integrating the findings of each step will yield managers a more comprehensive view of the impacts of immigration on a particular community.

DEMONSTRATING THE IMPACT ANALYSIS: A CASE STUDY

In addition to a theoretical presentation of the impact model and necessary statistical methods, this book uses the experiences of a major metropolitan area host community, Miami, Florida, to demonstrate the utility and findings of the model. The selected community has undergone one of the most intensive, high-profile, and long-term immigration events in the United States since World War I. The region has been marked by both a relatively constant flow of legal and illegal immigration, and periodic massive immigration events that make estimation of impacts very difficult. Data collection for this case study include legal and illegal immigrant surveys, expert interviews, and archival data analysis on immigration and immigration effects over a thirty-year period.

The Dade County region and the City of Miami have experienced high levels of both documented and undocumented immigrants from a variety of countries, and the model allows the review of different effects among these groups. The total resulting data base is unique to the field of immigration research and allows comparison of the utility of alternative forecasting and data collection techniques, the evaluation of alternative municipal strategies for managing immigration, and the examination of variations in impact over time and across services and revenue sources.

The insights gained from an extensive review of a single community undergoing a series of recent immigration waves is invaluable. While the purpose of the case study is illustrative, the findings offer not only a description of the impact of immigration, but an example of how the results, dynamics, and expectations can be generalized and applied in other U.S. counties or cities.

However, as with any case study there are limitations to the generalizability of findings warranting review. For example, the impacts on local government are conditioned by the nature of the immigrant population. Since the largest group of documented and undocumented immigrants residing in Miami are Hispanic and Haitian, cities which experience flows from other nations and regions of the world may experience different results. That is, it cannot be assumed that Hispanics or Haitians provide the same net benefits and costs to a municipal government as a large Asian or Mexican population. Previous research suggests that the nature and characteristics of an immigrant population play a large role in determining impacts (Tienda and Jensen, 1986).

Irrespective of the demographic and social characteristics of a particular immigrant group, the techniques of impact analysis employed in this book are applicable across local governments. In fact, the methodology can be applied regardless of the size of the community, the nature of the immigrants, and the skill level of local administrators.

SUMMARY

Previous research on immigration focuses largely on the fiscal impacts for federal and state governments, neglecting the effects on local governments as essential providers of services to immigrants. This gap in the research is particularly noticeable when viewing the historical relationship between immigration and city development. While the development of urban jurisdictions has been shaped by incoming immigrant groups, immigration policy remains the purview of the federal government.

This chapter presented four assumptions, based on the immigration literature, that address the research question, "Do immigrants (both legal and undocumented) pay more local taxes and fees then they consume in local government services?" The chapter then introduced a seven-step model for analyzing immigration impacts. The model provides the framework of this book and offers a systematic process for collecting and interpreting quantitative and qualitative data that will assist local government decision makers in planning and managing the effects of immigration. A case study focusing on the experiences of Miami, Florida, will illustrate the utility of the model and its products.

NOTES

1. Shortly after passage of the act, however, Congress repealed the law due to pressure from organized labor and the economic recession of the 1880s.

2. In compiling these references, a number of guidelines were followed to ensure proper coverage or research:

  a. Major books, journals, convention proceedings, and monographs which were recent and easily accessible were used.

  b. All of the material dealt specifically with the impact of immigration on various sectors of U.S. society.

  c. The review was limited to studies conducted in the United States or research findings that pertained to particular U.S. components.

3. Heer's analysis determined that, on average, undocumented and documented alien participation rates were less than that of natives for federal and state services such as food stamps, medical assistance, public housing, AFDC, and unemployment programs, while contributing roughly similar dollar amounts in federal withholding taxes (income taxes). Overall, Heer concluded that immigrants provide a net benefit to government.

4. Currently, the Unfunded Mandate Reform Act of 1995 requires termination of unfunded mandates which are duplicative, obsolete, or lack practicality and suspension of those unfunded mandates, not vital to public health and safety, that are determined to compound the financial difficulties of state and local governments.

5. The process of classifying immigrants by year of legal entry into the United States can be used as a successful technique for analyzing assimilation patterns of various immigrant groups. Simon (1984) determined that legal immigrant families which resided for longer periods of time in the United States were more likely to provide financial benefits than more recently arriving legal immigrants.

6. These methods are not without limitations. First, use of service-provider data may only capture a portion of undocumented alien usage of public service and may underestimate the use of other local government services, such as fire, police, and parks. Nor will it suffice to document the total illegal population. Further, historical analysis for longitudinal purposes necessitates generating assumptions of immigrant characteristics that previous official data do not provide.

CHAPTER 2 _____

Documenting Immigration

Fundamental to understanding the relationships between immigration, municipal service demands, and revenue capacity is enumerating the immigration population residing in a particular municipality. This first step is essential in establishing baseline information for both estimates of fiscal impact and the success of municipal efforts to manage immigration. However, it is very difficult to accurately enumerate immigration levels. The inability stems from both the nature and timing of official immigration data and the various terms used to describe the immigrant population.

This chapter begins with a brief examination of definitional issues which potentially muddle the collection of data relating to immigration. Then, the various techniques for enumerating both legal and undocumented immigrants are presented. Having established a benchmark that estimates both immigrant populations, the next section describes and analyzes various demographic characteristics. The utility of disaggregating immigration data is based, in part, on the assumption that demographic characteristics (such as age, gender, occupation, and family status) are related to service usage and revenue generation. The Miami case study demonstrates the strengths and weaknesses of the techniques. In addition, the case study exemplifies how difficult this process is, and how one can anticipate and deal proactively with many of the data limitations confronting researchers.

TERMINOLOGY AND IMMIGRATION

To many researchers not intimately familiar with the numerous terms used to describe immigration, appropriate data collection can be difficult. The definitions of immigrant and refugee from a stipulative vantage, for example, are very different from those used by the INS. Since the INS is the federal agency charged with implementing U.S. immigration policy and enforcing immigration laws, as well as generating and disseminating statistics on immigration, these distinctions are important. Commonly, an immigrant is anyone residing in this country whose origin of birth is another country. However, the federal government and the INS use a much narrower lexical definition. According to the INS, any alien admitted to the United States as a lawful, permanent resident is an immigrant. Therefore, immigrants are only those individuals accorded the legal privilege of residing permanently in the United States.

Similarly, the common definition of a refugee is anyone seeking residency in this country claiming economic hardship or fear of political persecution in their home country. The INS again uses a much narrower definition of refugee which requires supporting evidence: An alien admitted to the United States on the basis of a "well-founded fear of persecution" based on race, religion, nationality, or social or political ties qualifies as a refugee. Complicating this classification scheme is the physical location of the individual seeking refuge. If an applicant is located in the United States at the time they request refugee status, they are considered an asylee. A person requesting asylum who is physically located outside the borders of the United States is considered a refugee.

Another source of conflict, or at minimum difficulty, in determining the number of immigrants residing in the United States is the identification of foreign nationals. Potential immigrants can originally enter the country without identifying their true intentions. The INS currently classifies whether an individual is a foreign national based on what the individual claims as the intent of their visit. This process leaves much room for speculation. A foreign national may, for example, be classified as an asylee, temporary visitor, or undocumented alien.

If the visitor is still within the legal umbrella of their visa but has applied for asylum, they are officially recognized as an asylee. However, a foreign national may chose not to make their plan to stay beyond their visa known to immigration officials, or may have simply entered the country without documentation, and thus become undocumented.[1] Therefore, similar to hidden levels of unreported crime, there exists an ever present but hidden figure of immigration. This net annual population gain is never fully documented by official INS statistics. The actual number of immigrants, asylees, foreign nationals, or refugees in any particular jurisdiction can be expected to vary substantially from official estimates due to the disparity between INS-defined classifications and common usage. Figure 2.1 lists the commonly used terms related to immigration.

Employing a stipulative approach, this research defines an immigrant as any non-U.S. citizen who has resided or is currently residing in the United States, either legally or illegally, with the intent of maintaining residency for a period of time. The first component of the definition is not overtly difficult to understand. An immigrant is any individual who has lived or is currently living in the United States, whether that individual has been granted legal status or not, and is not recognized as a U.S. citizen. However, the more difficult part of the definition regards the intent to maintain residency. Under this rubric, foreign nationals are considered immigrants if the conditions of their temporary admissions violate the conditions of legal ingress. Therefore, students who violate their visa are considered immigrants for computational purposes.

Figure 2.1
Key Terms

ADJUSTMENT TO IMMIGRANT STATUS: Procedure granted by the Immigration Reform and Control Act of 1986 and INA allowing certain aliens already resident in the United States to apply for temporary-resident status or apply for immigrant status. When an alien applies for such adjustment, they are counted as an immigrant as of the date of adjustment, even though they may have resided in the United States for a given number of years.
ADMISSION: The legal ingress of an alien or a citizen into the United States through an officially recognized port of entry.
ALIEN: Any individual who is not a national or citizen of the United States.
ASYLEE: Any individual physically present in the United States or located at a port of entry who is unable or unwilling to return to their country of nationality. An asylee is defined similar to a refugee, the only difference is the location of the alien when seeking application; the asylee is physically located in the United States, while a refugee is located outside the official borders of the United States.
EMIGRANT: Any person who vacates one country to reside in another country.
EXCLUDABLE ALIEN: An alien who may be denied legal admission into this country on grounds specified in the Immigration and Nationality Act.
ILLEGAL ALIEN: Any person entering the United States without inspection or with fraudulent documentation, or any person who enters the country legally but subsequently violates the terms and conditions of their visa.
IMMIGRANT: Any alien who is admitted to the United States as a lawful permanent resident and is accorded all the rights and privileges of such.
LABOR CERTIFICATION: This document certifies that there is either no adverse affect on the wages and working conditions of individuals currently employed in the United States or that there is a need in the workforce that is not currently being provided from the job pool, and grants temporary working status to aliens.
NATIONALITY: The country of an individual's citizenship.
NATURALIZATION: The granting of citizenship, through any means, to a noncitizen.

Figure 2.1 (continued)

```
NONIMMIGRANT: Any individual who seeks temporary admission to
the United States for a specified period of time or for a
specific purpose.
PAROLEE: Any alien granted non-formal admission to the United
States for emergency reasons or humanitarian conditions.
PERMANENT RESIDENT ALIEN: Any individual entering the United
States under an immigrant visa, refugee, asylee, or
nonimmigrant visa but adjusted to resident status, who is
conferred all the rights and privileges of citizenship.
REFUGEE: Any individual located outside their country of
nationality who is unable or unwilling to return to that
country for fear of prosecution based on nationality, race,
political beliefs, religion, or membership in a particular
group.
REPATRIATION: The restoration or return of an individual to
the country of birth or citizenship.
TEMPORARY RESIDENT: Any alien who is granted adjustment to
temporary-resident status for a specified period of time.
Temporary residents must adjust to permanent-resident status
within a prescribed period of time or be subject to
deportation.
UNDOCUMENTED ALIEN: Any individual who does not possess proper
documentation granting legal entry into the United States.
Undocumented aliens are typically considered illegal aliens;
however, they could also be someone who has temporarily
misplaced their passport or other official documentation.
```

Within these diffuse parameters, immigration can be defined as the physical act of moving residency between nation-states. If individuals live in the United States and entered the nation illegally, but have sought out legal channels to seek permanent residency, they are considered status adjustments. During the long application process, these individuals are neither legal immigrants or undocumented aliens. They are in a legal limbo. Only when they are officially recognized as residents do they become legal immigrants. If official status is not granted, these individuals must either leave the country or become illegal immigrants.

In contrast to immigration, migration is defined as the movement between areas within the nation, for instance, between Florida and Texas. Emigration, as the inverse of immigration, is the act of locating to another country, either an individual's original birth country or another, from the country where the immigrant resides.

ESTIMATING DOCUMENTED IMMIGRANTS

Legal immigration levels for local governments can be calculated using data from the U.S. Immigration and Naturalization Service. This information is readily accessible through various INS publications. One of the first difficulties encountered with the data is that the information contained in INS data bases varies across time periods. For example, reported figures between 1953, the first year official numbers were gathered, and 1972 do not separate legal immigrants from individuals who sought status adjustment after arrival. The inclusion of status adjustments seriously misrepresents immigrant arrivals in any given year, because a large number of individuals adjust to immigrant status several years after original entry.[2]

To deal with this limitation in our case study, the City of Miami immigration totals for each year prior to 1972 were estimated and shifted to year of entry (rather than year of adjustment). This method assigns immigrants to a particular jurisdiction based on what immigrants reported as their intended residency if granted status adjustment. This is particularly important for the dominant Cuban immigrant population during the period. Given that location patterns did not vary substantially during the period (i.e., Cubans typically lived in Miami prior to seeking adjustment), the assumption that they resided in the community prior to seeking adjustment does not artificially inflate estimates. In contrast, adjustment levels for other nationalities were anticipated to be minor and assumed to be insignificant. They were included with immigration totals for the year they adjusted.

For the period 1972 to 1982, legal immigration can be directly estimated using INS immigration data, either in written form, tape, or on disk. The information provided by the INS includes basic demographic data on all arriving immigrants and immigrant status adjustments in a given year. However, detailed location variables are not easily extracted from this information, and care should be taken when using this information.

Fortunately, the 1983–1995 INS immigrant data include zip code identifiers. City and county totals for legal and adjusted-status immigrants can be calculated by summing totals for all county and city zip codes under review. These figures represent a relatively stable base to document the number of legal immigrants in a particular jurisdiction. Further, this process is vital, since the Immigration Reform and Control Act of 1986 granted amnesty to many illegal aliens who resided in the United States prior to 1986.

Immigrant Status Adjustment

When attempting to determine the number of immigrants residing in a particular municipality, as well as analyzing how long they have lived in the community, it is necessary to account for individuals who originally entered under illegal provisions (such as students), but sought status adjustment after arrival. This information is necessary to collect, because there may be different levels of financial impact between legal and illegal immigrant groups. To isolate the effect of residency status, those individuals who entered under one set of legal circumstances and then sought official reclassification through the INS must be allocated to the year of original entry.

If an individual enters a particular community as a foreign visitor, with or without the intention of seeking legal immigrant status but with the intent of remaining in the municipality, determining the year of entry becomes important. If we fail to capture these individuals, then the total financial impact of aliens may be artificially suppressed. Therefore, determining the year of entry becomes a vital task for completing the impact analysis.

Allocation of an immigrant to year of entry and including them in entry totals for the city assumes that the immigrant does not change municipality (or county) between entry and adjustment. For most immigrants, this is a fairly safe assumption, since the average time between entry and officially seeking adjustment is less than two years.

Unfortunately, this assumption would be incorrect in the case study for the 1980 Cuban–Haitian entrants and perhaps even more problematic for the 1994 Cuban influx. The majority of Cubans involved in the Mariel Boat Lift of 1980 did not adjust their legal status until 1987, and 1980 Haitian entrants tended to adjust in 1988. Further complicating the count, many of these individuals have changed their residency between entry and adjustment, due in part to the lengthy lag between arrival and adjustment.

The City of Miami influx of documented immigrants (e.g., immigrants with green cards who have designated Miami as their permanent mailing address) has been somewhat erratic (see Table 2.1). During major peaks in the early 1960s, late 1960s, and early 1970s, the number of immigrants approached 27,000 in a given year, culminating in 1980 with 49,160 immigrants. Between the peaks, legal immigration to Miami during the 1980s declined to a still sizable 6,000 to 7,000 immigrants per year.

The erratic nature of the data is caused primarily by variations in the flow of immigrants who adjust to legal immigrant status once they reside in the United States. The flow of newly arriving immigrants who enter with legal immigrant status has witnessed a fairly stable growth trend. Since 1972, the first year the new arrival component can be separated from the status adjustment, immigrant numbers ranged from 3,085 to a high of 7,350 in 1980, then to a low of 2,582 in 1988. The yearly amounts may be overstated somewhat, because prior to 1983 statistics are only available on immigrants designating Miami or Dade County as their final destination.[3] Fortunately, there is an underlying and relatively stable pattern among this segment of documented immigrants from which baseline estimates can unfold.

Table 2.1 also reveals that the arrival of aliens who subsequently adjust to legal residency status while residing in Miami is less stable (status adjustments). This group includes aliens who arrive with temporary visas, such as students, visitors, and, most important in explaining various peaks and valleys, refugees. Most of the documented immigrants to the City of Miami initially arrived with nonimmigrant status and adjusted to permanent residency later. The number of such adjustments peaked in the early 1970s, which represents Cuban refugees arriving via the air bridge in the 1950s and 1960s, followed by a second peak in 1980 which represents the Mariel–Cuban Boat Lift and Haitian entrants.

Table 2.1
City of Miami Documented Immigration Totals by Year

Year	New Arrivals	Status Adjustments	Total Documented
56			5509
57			5263
58			5512
59			13203
60			24073
61			21437
62			34106
63			19971
64			10366
65			12833
66			25301
67			27282
68			29410
69			26237
70			25893
71			25700
72	3085	11471	14556
73	3474	5374	8848
74	3787	15631	19418
75	3303	11462	14765
76	3466	4574	8040
77	5429	3387	8816
78	5319	2540	7859
79	6099	3355	9454
80	7350	41810	49160
81	6709	1943	8652
82	5740	1385	7125
83	2578	1171	3749
84	2754	843	3597
85	2936	607	3543
86	2863	409	3272
87	2609	158	2767
88	2582	74	2656

The drop in the number of adjustment immigrants in the mid- to late 1980s is misleading, as aliens entering during these years have not had time to adjust to permanent resident status. Depending on the legal disposition of the recent Cuban and Haitian influx, a large number of aliens entering during this period may eventually be granted immigrant status. Moreover, recent political changes in Eastern Europe and Central America have reduced the current refugee flow and have led to fewer grants of political asylum. INS has indicated that, because of the political changes, it will review cases that have been tentatively granted political asylum but have not yet completed the process.

Eventually, INS may revoke the grant of political asylum to many aliens seeking status adjustment. In addition, other alien groups, such as Central Americans, may be admitted under different legislative provisions. Recent court rulings require INS to reexamine Guatemalan and Salvadorian asylum and farm worker amnesty denials, which may result in a significant increase in adjustments over the next decade.

Status Adjustment and Municipal Management

The erratic nature and importance of adjustment immigrants in the over-all flow of immigration creates special problems for the municipal manager trying to anticipate increases in service demands. In comparison, aliens arriving with immigrant status have, during the long immigrant visa process, had an opportunity to plan their arrival. They come with a work permit, so they can immediately seek regular employment. Because they are entering through a legal process with numerical limitations in many cases, the flow is relatively stable and information on the number arriving is more accessible.

In contrast, refugees or parolees are likely to need more services and have more difficulty adapting, because they often come less prepared and frequently are legally barred from seeking employment. Moreover, they are more difficult to anticipate and track. Both groups of immigrants come, at least in part, in reaction to political and economic events, but the asylum and refugee adjustment cases are particularly motivated by social, economic, and political disruptions. Permission to immigrate is, by definition, given retrospectively to those adjusting status, and therefore estimating the number or timing of arrival is problematic.

In sum, it is difficult for the municipal manager to know how many people within their jurisdiction fit into the adjustment category. Many years may pass between entry and final adjustment to immigrant status. During this transition there is no official information on the location of the alien or the financial impact on the municipality.

This matter is further complicated in that aliens may have moved within the United States between entry and adjustment. The adjustment numbers indicated in Table 2.1 represent the number of aliens who arrived in a given year and eventually adjusted to immigrant status. The table shows 41,810 adjustment immigrants arrived in Miami in 1980. Actually, the bulk of these immigrants arrived in the Mariel Boat Lift, and many were initially resettled out of the city. Apparently, most of these individuals moved back to Miami prior to adjusting status. The bulk of status adjustments in this group occurred in 1987 for Cubans and in 1988 for Haitians. The actual influx into the City of Miami of the initially resettled aliens occurred between 1980 and 1988 and was less precipitous on local municipalities than Table 2.1 suggests.

DOCUMENTING THE UNDOCUMENTED:
FIVE ESTIMATION TECHNIQUES

If measuring past and anticipating future legal documented immigration is risky, estimating the level of undocumented immigration is very difficult. This task, however, is crucial for studying municipal impacts. Indeed, the estimation of this segment of the immigration population is likely to be a more important step for some municipalities. Undocumented aliens are foreign nationals who enter and remain in the United States without contacting immigration authorities or foreign nationals who violate the conditions of their temporary visas (such as overstaying a student visa). The undocumented, by definition, are not recognized in official INS statistics because the INS does not know they are in the country. Moreover, the undocumented have a clear incentive to remain "invisible." If INS discovers them, they are subject to deportation. Nevertheless, undocumented immigration may be a major source of demand on municipal services. Therefore, managing and providing services requires estimation of the undocumented. Several techniques have been advanced to estimate this population, but none of them are entirely satisfactory (General Accounting Office, 1994).[4]

Five indirect estimating techniques are offered here: (1) legal immigration weighted using Warren and Passel's ratio estimates of undocumented residents, (2) adjusting Warren and Passel's national ratios to reflect local conditions, (3) changes in school enrollment by foreign nationals, (4) asylum requests made to INS, and (5) changes in recorded U.S. births by foreign-national women to estimate the overall foreign-born population specific to a particular area.

Using Census Data to Estimate the Number of Undocumented Residents

One technique to estimate the undocumented population is based on official census data. Census data can be used to estimate the proportion of undocumented aliens counted in the 1980 and 1990 censuses based on the number of legal immigrants enumerated. While neither the 1980 nor 1990 censuses directly asked the immigration status of foreign nationals, these data have been used to estimate the number of undocumented aliens in the United States by year of entry and nationality (Warren and Passel, 1987). The estimate is derived by subtracting the number of legal immigrants of a particular nationality entering during a specified period listed on alien registration reports from the number of aliens counted in the 1980 census of that nationality who reported entering during that period.[5]

The estimate of illegal aliens uses national immigration figures to calculate the proportion of undocumented to legal immigration by year of entry and nationality. This proportion is then used to derive an estimate of undocumented immigration based on known levels of legal immigration. The formula developed for the City of Miami is as follows:[6]

$$UNDOC_1 = \%UNDOC/TOTIMM * LOCATION$$

where

   $UNDOC_1$ = Total undocumented immigration for a given period for a given region
         of the United States.

   $\%UNDOC$ = The proportion of undocumented aliens determined by Warren and
         Passel's computation, by nationality and location.

   $TOTIMM$ = National immigration totals for legal aliens in a given year.

   $LOCATION$ = Immigrants by nationality identified by zip code for census figures.

The simplicity of the equation merits its use, and concurrently limits its directness. That is, the dependent variable is the estimate of undocumented aliens residing in a jurisdiction. This figure is based in part on the assumption that Warren and Passel's estimates accurately reflect current conditions (Table 2.2). If these assumptions are correct, then the application of the equations is relatively straightforward and unambiguous.

Adjusting National Ratios to Reflect Local Conditions

Use of Warren and Passel's proportional estimates of undocumented aliens by nationalities, and applying them to a specific local government like the City of Miami, is based in part on the assumption that the percentage of undocumented aliens for each nationality residing in the United States is equivalent to the proportion of undocumented aliens for that nationality residing in a particular locale. The potential limitation of using national estimates of undocumented residents to study local impacts is that the immigrant mix on the local level may not be similar to the mix on the national level. To account for local conditions, a second method has been developed using Warren and Passel's ratios, which provides a more realistic and accurate estimate of undocumented aliens residing in the case study area.

In this estimate, the total number of undocumented aliens from various nationalities is subtracted from the Census Bureau count of total foreign-born residents of that nationality (Table 2.2). The difference represents undocumented aliens for each nationality, and the sum of undocumented aliens across nationalities represents the total number of undocumented aliens counted in the 1980 census. Both the INS and census data must be adjusted for underreporting prior to calculating total undocumented residents. Warren and Passel (1987) provide a measure of the proportion underreporting for each nationality, based on an analysis of yearly registration data and annual data on immigrants admitted during specific years,

Table 2.2
Undocumented Population of the City of Miami by Region and Nationality: 1980

Origin	Miami Alien Population 1980 census (Adjusted)[1]	Aliens Registered By INS 1980 (Adjusted)[2]	Undocumented Aliens Miami 1980[3]	Percent Undocumented Miami 1980[4]	United States 1980[5]
Africa	1604	736	868	54%	44%
Asia	8779	6349	2430	28%	12%
Europe	24920	17584	7336	29%	12%
N. America	294730	240602	54128	18%	40%
Canada	5193	3787	1406	27%	10%
Mexico	3814	2000	1814	48%	49%
Guatemala	1753	1254	499	28%	48%
Salvador	1514	776	738	49%	57%
Cuba	226262	201570	24692	11%	7%
Haiti	13859	3527	10332	75%	57%
Jamaica	13571	9950	3621	27%	25%
Other	28765	17738	11027	38%	
Oceania	452	176	276	61%	40%
S. America	39923	25826	14097	35%	28%
Columbia	16731	12314	4417	26%	22%
Other	23192	13512	9680	42%	31%
Total	370406	291274	79132	21%	28%

[1]1980 census adjusted for misreports of citizenship using Warren and Passel's (1987) technique.
[2]1980 INS registration data adjusted for underreporting using Warren and Passel's (1987) technique.
[3]Total aliens less documented aliens.
[4]Undocumented aliens divided by total aliens.
[5]Warren and Passel (1987).

deaths during those years, documented alien emigrants, and naturalization. They suggest underreporting ranges from under 9 percent for aliens from Spain to almost 48 percent for Haitians.

These proportions are used to adjust the City of Miami INS data upward. Use of national underreport proportions to adjust for local underreporting makes the assumption that underreporting by legal aliens was typical of nationwide levels. If underreporting was higher, the result is an underestimate of the undocumented population. Conversely, if local underreporting is lower than the national average, the undocumented population will be overestimated.

Warren and Passel correct for misreported citizenship by recalculating the number of naturalized citizens based on the number of immigrants naturalized since 1960 with allowance for death and emigration. The recalculated naturalized citizen totals are then subtracted from the number of foreign-born persons counted in the census, yielding an estimate of the alien population. The proportions of misreported citizenship calculated for various nationalities are used to adjust the Miami census count of the alien population. These adjustments do not account for an undercount of undocumented aliens in the census.

A working application of these estimations is provided for the City of Miami in Table 2.2. Of the 370,406 aliens in Miami enumerated in the 1980 census, 79,132 (21%) were undocumented. This compares with 28 percent nationally. The proportion of undocumented aliens is lower in Miami, in part, because of differences in the composition of the immigrant population. This finding indicates the importance of adjusting estimates to reflect local patterns. Relying solely on national estimates to project local circumstances could produce severely biased results and generate inaccurate or faulty conclusions. Therefore, it is vital for local administrators to sensitize national standards with local characteristics. Figures then represent a much more realistic picture for policy directions.

This is exemplified in our case study. Nationally, immigration has been dominated by Mexicans, while in the City of Miami, immigration has been dominated by Cubans. About 40 percent of the U.S. foreign-born population in 1980 and 1990 was Mexican, while in Miami, Mexicans made up only a little over 1 percent of the alien population counted for both periods. On the other hand, Cubans accounted for 5 percent of the overall foreign-born population, but over 61 percent of Miami immigration. According to Warren and Passel's ratio estimates, Mexican immigrants include a relatively high proportion of undocumented aliens. In contrast, the Cuban-born population includes a very low proportion of undocumented aliens (about 7% nationally and 11% locally). If Mexican and Cuban aliens are removed from the calculation, Miami actually had a much higher percentage of undocumented resident aliens than the nation as a whole (38% for Miami versus 20% for the nation).

The proportion of undocumented aliens varies substantially across nationalities. Nearly 75 percent of the Haitian immigrants in Miami are undocumented (57% nationally) compared to only about 11 percent of the Cuban aliens. Although the Cuban population had the smallest proportion of undocumentation of any nationality, the population of Cubans in Miami is so large that the Cuban undocumented population (24,692) remains greater than that of any other local nationality. According to this estimation method, the Cuban undocumented population represents nearly one-third of the total undocumented population.[7]

While Warren and Passel provide a plausible estimation approach, addition techniques can further reduce the limitations of official census and INS data in enumerating the undocumented population. These techniques have been applied in previous studies examining the effects of undocumented aliens and their associated impacts on government. The techniques are not intended to provide definitive figures that can be used to justify policy, but instead are methods useful in substantiating or augmenting figures generated from census and INS data.

School Data for Estimation Purposes

Public school data provide a rich source by which undocumented aliens can be estimated. In Florida, public school systems are required to service all school-age children, regardless of immigration status. The Florida school system has maintained excellent records since 1983 on the foreign-born student population.

Yearly data on new enrollments by refugees and undocumented foreign-born students can be used to estimate undocumented immigration.[8] The enrollment data are adjusted in accordance with the percentage of legal immigrants that are school aged (the age distribution of legal immigrants is obtained from INS immigrant records).[9] In 1989–1990, approximately 28 percent of the legal immigrants were school age. There were 7,963 new students classified as refugees or undocumented aliens entering Miami public schools during this period.

If the proportion of school-age undocumented aliens is similar to that of legal immigrants (28%), then based upon the 3,066 children enrolled in Miami schools in 1989, an estimated 10,949 undocumented and refugee aliens lived in the area during 1989. This estimate is used as the base figure for total 1989 undocumented population residing in the city (allowing for a minor time lag between arriving and registering for school).

Unfortunately, the school-based total immigration calculation does not consider foreign-born children in private schools. Yields, therefore, may be closer to the lower end of the continuum of total immigration than if all foreign-born students were included. The consequences of this omission can be examined by looking at available statistics from the largest component of local private education, the Catholic educational system.

Statistics were available on the number of Haitian and the number of Nicaraguan students enrolled in both private and public school systems.[10] In 1989, 222 Nicaraguan students were enrolled in Catholic schools, which is a little over 1 percent of the 18,331 Nicaraguan-born students enrolled in Miami public schools. Haitian students in Catholic schools numbered 872, nearly 17 percent of the 5,209 Haitians enrolled in public schools. Overall, Catholic school enrollments in Miami were 19,816, or 7 percent of the 279,554 students in the public school system. Combining the data from both public and private school enrollments, roughly 11,000 undocumented students reside in the city.

Political Asylum Applications Filed with INS

Data from INS Form G23-3, Supplement A, "Asylum Cases Filed with District Directors, pursuant to Section 208 INA," provide a third source for estimating undocumented immigration. An asylee is any individual who entered the country under provisions that did not qualify as permanent immigrant status, and who has since contacted official authorities to seek asylum. These individuals most typically arrived in the United States during periods of large migration of similar individuals from their host country. They were unable or unwilling to pursue legal channels in their country, for fear either of persecution or reprisal, and felt compelled to enter the United States through any channel possible.

Further, asylum cases frequently represent multiple applicants. According to the Miami district office of the INS, an asylum case, on average, represents 1.5 to 1.75 individuals. The statistics in this study use an estimate of individuals rather than cases, based on the assumed 1.75 persons per application. For administrators grappling with their particular community, these figures can be gathered through regional INS offices, either by phone or personal interviews with regional directors.

The ratio provided by the district office used in this study proves to be relatively accurate when this number is compared to findings of the other estimating processes. Moreover, various sources available on the local level provide fruitful means of evaluating recommendations. Comparing density figures produced by the Census Bureau, local housing demands, building permits, and water and sewer consumption all provide substantive benchmarks to judge the usefulness of the figures reported by INS. The asylum data are compiled by INS for the entire State of Florida. The Miami portion is estimated for various nationalities and nationality groupings based on the percentage of total asylum cases filed statewide (see Table 2.3).

Table 2.3
Political Asylum Applications Filed: City of Miami INS District Office

Year	Dade County	City of Miami
84	11351	3645
85	8946	2828
86	10454	3188
87	12274	3741
88	7970	2358
89	30956	9083

These figures are computed periodically, and are readily available to local administrators.

While INS asylum application data proved useful in calculating a base level of undocumented immigration, INS (through an interview with Mr. Cauler of the district Political Asylum division, June 12, 1990) notes particular limitations:

- The accumulative numbers are for in-house use and are not systematically checked for accuracy (this was confirmed based on the fact that individual nationality totals do not sum to the grand total).

- Applications received do not include cases that were immediately rejected or discouraged by the officer completing the form—indicating a potential for undercounting this population.

- There is a backlog at INS in processing the applications, thus delaying their inclusion in the received data.

Furthermore, many undocumented aliens never apply for asylum. In fact, application for asylum may be based as much, or more, on perceptions of probable success than on the number of undocumented immigrants in the community. Since an alien can file the application at any time after entry, there may be a relatively long delay between entry and application.

As a consequence, the asylum data clearly underestimate the undocumented population, and application patterns may be somewhat misleading because of their relation to INS policy. (For this reason, we used the upper bound estimates provided by INS.) But the statistics do provide an indication of broad trends in undocumented immigration, and may suggest the time horizon between entry and adjustment.

Births by the Foreign-Born Population

The fifth technique for estimating overall undocumented immigration is based on births by foreign-born women. The State of Florida maintains aggregate data on the number of births per year. The data are divided into various categories based on the mother's race and country of birth, and are cross-listed with the mother's reported residence at childbirth.

For the particular nationalities relative to the City of Miami, country-of-birth categories include the United States, Cuba, Canada, Mexico, and the rest of the world. Race is categorized as white, black, and other. In this case study, the data were grouped into six categories: Cuban, Canadian, Mexican, rest-of-world white, rest-of-world black, and rest-of-world other. The birth data are used to index foreign-born population census figures and subsequent population totals are calculated based on changes in the number of births.

The proportional change in births in a given year, using 1980 births as a base, was calculated for each race and country-of-birth category. The proportion change from 1980 as calculated with the birth data was used to weight the census count, yielding a yearly estimate of the total foreign-born population for each category. The following equation was used to generate these figures:

$$\text{BIRTHS} = 1980\text{CNT} * \%\text{FOREBRTH}$$

where

> BIRTHS = Total births of foreign-born children in a given time frame.
>
> 1980CNT = Documented foreign-born nationals residing in the municipality and enumerated in the 1980 census.
>
> %FOREBRTH = Proportion change in foreign births since 1980, adjusted by nationality and compared to immigrant birth trends of the same nationality the previous five years.

The category estimates were summed, generating a yearly estimate of the total foreign-born population. Year-to-year changes in the foreign-born population were then calculated and compared with the total legal and adjusted immigration levels. The difference is the estimate of undocumented immigration.

Municipal estimates of total foreign-born population and the yearly change in this population are calculated in the same manner. Since the census data do not break down population estimates by nationality at the municipal level, INS registration data were used to calculate Miami's total in each category. Assuming the same proportions exist as for documented aliens, this percentage was used to weight the census estimates for Miami.

The calculation and subsequent indexing of foreign-born population census figures assumes that the birthrate within the national groupings remained constant between 1980 and 1988. In one group, rest-of-world white (a group combining Europe, Central America, South America [except for Guiana], and some of the non-Cuban Caribbean aliens), this assumption was problematic. Therefore, estimates of the change in birthrates across the period were developed and alternative estimations of the foreign-born population totals were estimated.

As was the case with the school-based estimates, there is a lag in the estimates derived from births to foreign-born mothers. The rigors of immigration and difficulties associated with settling into a new community may delay pregnancy for immigrants (and migrants). This may be offset by the incentive for undocumented immigrants to give birth to a U.S.-born citizen to presumably improve their chances of obtaining legal status under the rubric of family reunification.

The use of births by foreign-born mothers to index 1980 foreign-born population tallies provides an opportunity to estimate and examine changes in the overall foreign-born population. Changes in this population reflect immigration as well as migration from other parts of the United States, mortality, and out-migration. The unadjusted population and change estimates are based on 1980 and 1990 census counts indexed yearly by the number of foreign-born women giving birth in that year. The adjusted population and change estimates are also based on indexed census counts, but adjustments have been made to account for estimated changes in the birthrate.

Foreign population estimates are not pure measures of immigration, but rather reflect change in the level of foreign-born aliens. Immigration is only one component of this change. The change also includes several factors which reduce the foreign-born population, such as emigration to other countries, out-migration to other cities, and deaths of foreign-born aliens.[11] Conversely, migration from other parts of the United States by foreign-born persons can increase this population independent of immigration. The magnitude of the effect of these components on estimates depends on the degree to which the number of women bearing children in a given year are affected by these factors.

The pattern of change for Miami is intriguing (see Table 2.4). The early 1980s demonstrate a relatively large net increase in foreign-born population. Primarily, this increase is attributable to nearly 37,000 foreign-born residents (based on the adjusted population estimate) from 1980 to 1982. These figures reflect, in large part, the Mariel influx. Levels drop in the middle of the decade, actually becoming a net outflow when Cubans are included in the estimate, and rise toward the end of the decade. There are increases of about 10,000 from 1986 to 1987 and over 35,000 from 1987 to 1988, based on the more conservative adjusted estimate, and a total increase of just shy of 65,000 for the two-year period, based on the unadjusted estimate.

When Cubans are included in the estimate, the pattern is less stable. Inclusion of the Cubans more than doubles the estimated increase in the foreign-born population for 1980–1981 and 1981–1982. But the inclusion of Cubans results in an estimated net outflow of more than 10,000 foreign-born persons between 1983 and 1984. This is a trend which completely

Table 2.4
Yearly Change in Estimated Foreign-Born Population: City of Miami

Year	Unadjusted Change with Cubans	Unadjusted Change w/o Cubans	Birthrate Change with Cubans	Birthrate Change w/o Cubans
81	30183	13532	28253	11602
82	13649	6461	9343	2155
83	19526	9184	17832	7489
84	-7637	5347	-10558	2426
85	24346	16497	18675	10826
86	7459	16774	1774	11089
87	19273	25654	10458	16839
88	46677	34060	35373	22756

turns around for a one-year period (1984–1985), drops again, and then demonstrates sizable increases in the late 1980s and early 1990s.

The relatively complex pattern reflects the instability of influx and out-flow of the foreign-born population during the 1980s, particularly those of Cuban descent. The pattern suggests that substantial emigration (or, more likely, out-migration) occurred during the mid-1980s, possibly in reaction to the Mariel influx. This is most noteworthy among the established Cuban-born population. Immigration spikes are reflected by lagged increases in births by foreign-born mothers. But changes in in-migration, emigration, and out-migration are harder to document.[12]

Comparing Estimation Techniques

An interesting finding of the various estimating techniques is that, in most cases, large variation was produced (Table 2.5). Based on the findings of the case study, the most conservative technique is the unadjusted Warren and Passel technique (UNDOC1 in Table 2.5), while the technique that produced the largest estimate was based on the political asylum technique. Further, the variance between the school-based estimates and the asylum technique did not change substantially over the study period. As stated previously,

Table 2.5
Comparison of Undocumented Estimation Techniques and Foreign-Born Population Estimates: City of Miami

| | Undocumented Aliens | | | | Foreign Born Population | |
| | | | | | Total | |
Year	UNDOC1*	UNDOC2*	School Based Estimate	Political Asylum	Foreign Born	Adjusted for Birth Rate
72	1730	3708				
73	1986	3341				
74	2365	5019				
75	4775	4571				
76	2579	3705				
77	2393	4476				
78	2285	4556				
79	2898	4912				
80	1249	5054			245,354	245,354
81	2124	4908			275,537	273,607
82	1777	5249			289,186	282,950
83	977	3012	6537	6378	308,712	300,782
84	951	2685	6829	4949	301,076	290,224
85	935	2984	8591	5579	325,421	308,899
86		3704	9504	6547	332,880	310,673
87			9424	4127	352,152	321,130
88			15869	15895	389,929	356,503

*The UNDOC1 technique is derived from the unadjusted Warren and Passel's proportional estimates, while the UNDOC2 technique adjusts these figures to represent local conditions (see text for discussion).

given the inherent limitations of estimating the undocumented population residing in a particular municipality, a conservative approach should be pursued. Based on these findings, the census-based adjustments (UNDOC1 and UNDOC2 in Table 2.5) are used for calculation purposes throughout the remainder of this study. In those cases when a comparison is provided to analyze possible ranges, notification is given regarding the estimating technique employed.

A municipal manager must recognize that even well-done estimates of undocumented alien levels will be biased toward underestimation as more current years are examined. This means, unfortunately, that current-year estimates are likely to be the most undercounted and make current planning that much more difficult. A correction based upon local conditions, trends, and knowledge is recommended. Otherwise, services and resources will inevitably fall short, and spikes in local immigration will only be recognized in retrospect.

The overall effect of the various forces is a sizable increase in the foreign-born population in Miami during the 1980s according to the birth-index estimates. The unadjusted estimate suggests an overall increase in the foreign-born population of Miami from 30,188 in 1980, to 46,677 in 1988, an increase of nearly 16,500 persons during this period. The adjusted estimate suggests an increase from 13,532 in 1980, to 34,060 in 1988, an increase of more then 10,000 persons.

The data suggest a process reminiscent of the familiar ghettoization of cities around the country. The cities experience a constant influx of immigrants, but at the same time (and quite likely as a consequence of the influx), earlier immigrants move to other parts of the country. In the process, cities experience a net loss of wealth and, perhaps more important, a loss of stabilization, socialization, and adaptation. Cities become a "training ground" for newly arriving immigrants. These host communities provide training in language, social roles and responsibilities, use of government services, and other facets of life in America. Host communities bear the original costs of immigrant socialization, but are unable to reap any long-term benefits as established immigrants relocate.

Estimates derived from births by foreign-born mothers, school enrollment of foreign-born students, school enrollment of refugee and undocumented students, and the number of asylum applications processed by INS in a given year have been used to supplement census and INS data. All of these sources share a lagged-effect problem. They provide estimates which trail actual entry by varying amounts. For example, school enrollment may not occur for several years, and some undocumented children may never enroll. Changes in births may lag behind entry if the entrants delay pregnancy. Asylum applications may be made anytime after entry and are likely to increase during periods when asylums are perceived as more likely to be granted, regardless of the actual year of entry into the United States.

In addition, the impact of immigration on municipal services is not solely governed by the number of immigrants arriving in a given year. Immigrants vary in their needs and expectations of government support. They vary in their understanding of government, their ability to access government services, and their ability to communicate their needs through language skills and cultural norms.

The range and impact of such variations among immigrant groups is exemplified in the Miami case study. A review of the more significant demographic characteristics of documented immigrants for municipal service requirements follows. These dimensions are further applicable to any jurisdiction conducting similar multigroup impact analyses. They are not, however, the only characteristics impacting government that should be examined when evaluating impacts. The criteria only attempt to highlight the most significant characteristics and how managers can use this information for planning and policy making.

IMMIGRANT CHARACTERISTICS

Immigrant characteristics impact the level and nature of services demanded by both current aliens and longer-term immigrants. Therefore, it is important for anyone conducting an impact analysis to account for and analyze these differences. For the Miami case study, the characteristics of family status, occupation, and nationality are examined using INS data and, therefore, describe only documented immigrants.

Family Status

INS data reveal a fundamental shift in the proportion of documented immigrants in Miami who are part of the immediate or extended family of either another documented immigrant or a U.S. resident. In 1972, roughly 12 percent of all documented immigrants fell into immediate or extended family classifications; by 1988, nearly 95 percent of the documented immigrants were in these classifications (Table 2.6).[13]

The shift is the product of several factors. First, it reflects a reduction in the Cuban proportion of overall immigration. In the early 1970s, many of the immigrants were Cuban refugees who arrived with refugee status and were subsequently adjusted to immigrant status. The increase also reflects changes in immigration policy. Since 1952, with the passage of the McCarran–Walter Act, relatives of U.S. citizens and permanent residents have had an easier time gaining immigrant status. The McCarran–Walter Act instructed the INS to allocate 50 percent of available visas to relatives and 50 percent to immigrants in occupations with a shortage of U.S. workers. The Hart–Celler Act, passed in 1965, set up a preference system for eastern hemisphere immigrants, giving second preference to relatives of U.S. citizens and permanent resident aliens. In 1976, the preference system was expanded to

Table 2.6
Immigrant Status Based on Immediate or Extended Family Membership:
City of Miami Documented Immigrants

Year	Immediate Family		Extended Family		All Other	
	Count	Percentage	Count	Percentage	Count	Percentage
72	1506	10.3	171	1.2	12879	88.5
73	1982	22.4	215	2.4	6651	75.2
74	2136	11.0	259	1.3	17023	87.7
75	2001	13.6	252	1.7	12513	84.7
76	2164	26.9	358	4.5	5519	68.6
77	2647	30.0	1172	13.3	4997	56.7
78	3231	41.1	1730	22.0	2897	36.9
79	4609	48.8	2455	26.0	2389	25.3
80	4311	8.8	3057	6.2	41793	85.0
81	4646	53.7	2853	33.0	1153	13.3
82	4659	65.4	1576	22.1	888	12.5
83	2432	64.9	662	17.7	655	17.5
84	2202	61.2	976	27.1	420	11.7
85	2266	64.0	918	25.9	358	10.1
86	2452	75.0	565	17.3	254	7.8

include immigrants from the western hemisphere. This shift corresponds with a large increase in the proportion of Miami immigrants with family status between 1976 and 1981. The 1990 act shifted first-preference status from occupation to family reunification.

A final factor in the increase is a spiral effect from the changing demographic composition of the City of Miami. As the number of foreign-born citizens and permanent residents of Miami increases, more foreign relatives become eligible for immigration under the family status classifications. The preference for family members makes the past a prologue to future immigration. As the population eligible to bring in family members increases, so will the proportion and number of family members increase, and preexisting nationality patterns are reinforced. Over time, this creates a cyclical effect between family reunification and the transition of immigrants. First, the father, mother, son, or daughter immigrates. They enter through whatever means they can and obtain legal status as quickly as possible. Once established in a particular community, they request first preference status under the 1990 immigration act to reunite other family members, such as a spouse, dependent child, or grandparents. This process continues until the entire family is residing in a particular locale.

There are several implications for future immigration and municipal impacts for the Miami case study. The recent status adjustment of Mariel and Haitian entrants, as well as past adjustments of undocumented aliens through the Immigration Reform and Control Act of 1986, will (as undocumented immigrants become permanent residents and citizens) increase the local population eligible to bring in relatives. While the precise number of immigrants arriving may be controlled by quotas established by Congress, it is certain that the vast majority of forthcoming documented immigrants will be family members. Moreover, there is likely to be increased pressure on Congress to further expand "family reunification" visas to cope with the demand generated by aliens going through the legalization program. These forces may in turn lead to an increase in documented immigration.

The shift toward family status immigration also changes the impact of immigration on municipal services. Subsequent family members are more likely to be greeted with established support systems, potentially reducing the need for government intervention. On the other hand, these immigrants will be sooner and better positioned to demand public services. Their established relatives increase their knowledge of services that are available and provide assistance in accessing those programs.

Furthermore, immigrants arriving as relatives are likely to have relatively low labor-force participation rates. They will include a high proportion of minors, students, housewives, and retirees. As such, they will not, at least initially, contribute heavily to government revenues, but are likely to place a large demand on educational and recreational services.

Occupation

Immigrants are required to provide information on their occupation when applying for immigrant status. The occupation data are based on self-reports and may exaggerate the immigrant's true occupational status. However, the information does provide some indication of anticipated labor-force participation. The match of occupational characteristics to current or projected needs in a specific location is useful in predicting unemployment and resulting service utilization, as well as in predicting revenue impacts.

The distribution of immigrants across occupation categories is exhibited in Table 2.7. These findings indicate that the largest segment, a fairly consistent 60 percent of the immigrants, falls into the "no occupation" category. This category includes students, homemakers, retirees, and immigrants having no discernable occupational skills. The proportion of immigrants in this category varies little over the study period. It dips below 55 percent only in 1980, the year of the Mariel influx.

The largest component of the group classified as having no occupation are students (shown in Table 2.8). Students comprised over 26 percent of all documented immigrants in 1972, and this proportion climbed steadily (other than a drop to 18 percent in 1980) through the study period. By 1988, students made up more than 38 percent of all documented immigrants, although this proportion is likely to fall as aliens who arrived in 1988 adjust to immigrant status.

Table 2.7
Occupation of Immigrants: City of Miami Documented Immigrants

Year	Clerical and Sales	Laborer	Craft	Service	Professional and Technical	No Occupation
72	878	2391	905	868	1126	8388
73	546	1019	447	629	912	5295
74	1028	2525	1056	875	1646	12288
75	1014	2418	1042	655	1558	8079
76	508	951	392	422	909	4859
77	658	630	350	386	1433	5359
78	620	592	325	370	1219	4732
79	822	969	410	439	1191	5622
80	3148	9089	5153	8706	1951	21114
81	741	789	412	389	1162	5159
82	470	706	358	421	823	4345
83	259	378	231	301	341	2239
84	250	342	234	298	306	2168
85	254	352	266	331	291	2048
86	212	373	217	366	286	1817
87	164	262	161	284	259	1635
88	166	202	145	178	258	1707

Table 2.8
Occupation of Immigrants—No Occupation Category: City of Miami Documented Immigrants

	Homemaker		Student		Unemployed/ Retired		None	
Year	Count	Percentage	Count	Percentage	Count	Percentage	Count	Percentage
72	2619	18.0	3817	26.2	947	6.5	1005	6.9
73	1669	18.9	2383	26.9	682	7.7	561	6.3
74	3876	20.0	4848	25.0	2105	10.8	1459	7.5
75	2340	15.8	4587	31.1	574	3.9	578	3.9
76	1596	19.8	2460	30.6	377	4.7	426	5.3
77	1558	17.7	2999	34.0	365	4.1	437	5.0
78	1268	16.1	2729	34.7	354	4.5	381	4.8
79	1568	16.6	3107	32.9	476	5.0	471	5.0
80	7118	14.5	8541	17.4	2592	5.3	2863	5.8
81	1430	16.5	2892	33.4	394	4.6	443	5.1
82	1150	16.1	2419	34.0	356	5.0	420	5.9
83	633	16.9	1185	31.6	164	4.4	257	6.9
84	613	17.0	1152	32.0	214	5.9	189	5.3
85	511	14.4	1154	32.6	222	6.3	161	4.5
86	408	12.5	1131	34.6	165	5.0	113	3.5
87	313	11.3	1113	40.3	118	4.3	91	3.3
88	445	16.8	1099	41.4	37	1.4	126	4.7

Homemakers made up 17 percent of all immigrants in 1988. The proportion of homemakers held relatively constant at 14 to 20 percent through most of the study period. The unemployed and no occupation segment of this category produced much smaller proportions. In 1988, less than 2 percent of immigrants fell into the unemployed or retired category and 4 percent fell into the no occupation category. These percentages are down from highs of about 10 percent in each of the categories during the 1970s. Both categories include a much higher proportion of adjustment immigrants than new arrivals. As aliens arriving in the late 1980s and early 1990s adjust to immigrant status, the total proportion of immigrants falling into these categories will likely increase.

Under the professional and technical category, immigrants are spread across a variety of fields (Table 2.9). During the 1980s, the largest proportion were classified as managers. Presently, health professionals make up less than 3 percent of all documented immigrants, teachers less than 2 percent, managers less than 4 percent, and around 4 percent of immigrants fell into the category of other professionals (including lawyers, architects, researchers, engineers, counselors, etc.). The proportion of immigrants falling into the teaching category increased steadily over the study period, rising from less than 1 percent of all immigrants in 1972 to slightly over 1 percent in 1988.

The professional category comprises the second-largest number of immigrants (following, at some distance, the no occupation category) during the 1980s, with about 11 percent of all immigrants. In Miami, the Mariel Boat Lift of 1980 included a very low proportion of immigrants indicating professional skills (about 3.1 percent). The proportion of professionals peaked in the late 1970s at between 15 to 16 percent of all documented immigrants.

The laborer category has rather sharply declined in importance. The second-largest number of immigrants fell into this classification in the early

Table 2.9
Occupation of Immigrants—Professional Category: City of Miami Documented Immigrants

Year	Health Count	Health Percentage	Teacher Count	Teacher Percentage	Manager Count	Manager Percentage	Other Professional Count	Other Professional Percentage
72	159	1.1	82	0.6	403	2.8	482	3.3
73	158	1.8	58	0.7	328	3.7	368	4.2
74	300	1.5	70	0.4	485	2.5	791	4.1
75	247	1.7	55	0.4	502	3.4	754	5.1
76	204	2.5	44	0.5	436	5.4	225	2.8
77	216	2.5	77	0.9	812	9.2	328	3.7
78	148	1.9	95	1.2	585	7.4	391	5.0
79	180	1.9	91	1.0	497	5.3	423	4.5
80	487	1.0	187	0.4	614	1.2	663	1.3
81	167	1.9	132	1.5	442	5.1	421	4.9
82	128	1.8	72	1.0	315	4.4	308	4.3
83	59	1.6	43	1.1	127	3.4	112	3.0
84	51	1.4	42	1.2	115	3.2	98	2.7
85	50	1.4	37	1.0	114	3.2	90	2.5
86	51	1.6	24	0.7	121	3.7	90	2.8
87	61	2.2	25	0.9	100	3.6	73	2.6
88	52	2.0	27	1.0	70	2.6	109	4.1

1970s. Nearly 17 percent of immigrants in 1972 were classified in laborer occupations, but the proportion began falling in the late 1970s, and, other than a peak of nearly 20 percent in the Mariel year, was around 7 to 8 percent during the 1980s. In 1988, 7.3 percent of the documented immigrants were classified as laborers.

Nationality

Last, the change in the mix of immigrant nationalities across time has implications for immigration's impact on municipal services. Nationality effects the utilization of government services because some nationalities have better local support structures in place. These preexisting support systems can have both amplifying and dampening effects on service demands. They provide immigrants with alternatives to government services and simultaneously socialize immigrants concerning the utilization of government services.

In addition, some foreign governments provide a broad range of services, so that certain immigrants come with high expectations of government assistance. Others come from countries where governments are to be avoided (i.e., Haiti, prior to the U.S. invasion), and therefore those immigrants have a propensity to rely on other means for support. Further, nationalities tend to group in particular jurisdictions, forming enclaves that attract other immigrants. In addition, the language spoken by a particular nationality can indicate the ease of socialization and the ability of government to provide services. Finally, immigrants from underdeveloped countries are more likely to be poor and less educated, less likely to develop enclaves, have higher levels of labor-force participation, and are more likely to leave if they cannot find work.

In our case study, distribution based on nationality has changed over the last twenty years (Table 2.10). The bulk of immigrants to Miami have traditionally been from the Caribbean region. This remains true for legal immigrants, but the proportion of immigrants from the Caribbean declined from 82 percent in 1972, to 51 percent in 1988, and actually dropped below 50 percent for most of the 1980s. The drop in the proportion of Caribbean immigrants has been matched by an increase in the proportion of immigrants from South and Central America. The shift actually occurred in the late 1970s, and the proportions remained relatively stable in the 1980s, with the exception of the 1980 influx of immigrants from the Caribbean. Over the last few years, a small increase in the proportion of Asian immigrants has been identified, and they now make up nearly 8 percent of total legal immigration.

The regional pattern for total immigration (documented plus undocumented components) is very similar to the regional distribution pattern for documented immigration. As was true of documented immigration, the

Table 2.10
National Distribution Totals: Miami Documented Immigrants

Year	Africa	Asia	Central America	Caribbean	Europe	North America	Oceania	South America
72	57	467	400	11915	723	197	10	786
73	70	507	548	6030	633	147	19	895
74	59	478	641	16687	545	121	11	876
75	84	1008	579	11494	566	114	7	913
76	72	538	564	5232	506	179	16	934
77	92	607	740	4994	683	281	12	1406
78	52	570	905	3896	648	277	11	1498
79	74	562	1288	5100	554	211	13	1652
80	61	448	1071	45269	609	142	7	1553
81	63	465	1116	4612	561	162	8	1667
82	52	440	1097	3814	373	99	12	1238
83	12	129	627	2225	140	26	0	587
84	21	137	571	2203	127	28	1	507
85	14	127	667	2101	102	23	1	511
86	13	110	588	1889	117	32	2	522
87	15	143	594	1447	102	25	3	437
88	17	141	542	1530	68	12	1	345

Caribbean region becomes a relatively less important source of immigration over the study period and Central and South America become more important. The shift witnessed over the last decade in the location of immigrants may result in different impacts on the local level. Therefore, local administrators must account for changing immigration patterns to fully understand and capture the impacts different immigrant groups have on their municipality.

SUMMARY

Documenting various immigrant groups is vital to the success of analyzing the impact these individuals have on a particular municipality. This chapter discussed the availability of data (primarily using official census and INS sources) for estimating documented immigrants. To provide a more thorough and objective process than simply relying on national totals, various methods to estimate the number of illegal immigrants were presented. Sensitizing any data is a prerequisite to proper analysis. The methods using school data, political asylum applications, births by foreign-born women, and foreign-born population estimates were offered as techniques to sensitize data to local conditions. Next, the Miami case study illustrated the use of INS data to examine immigrant characteristics, including family status, occupation, and nationality.

The primary weakness of these estimation techniques for municipal managers and policy makers is their reliability over time. While providing relatively sound information to examine long-term historical trends or the impact of past large-scale immigration events, they do not provide good, current information because of the various lagged effects that have been discussed. Therefore, better sources of recent immigration activities are necessary. Chapter 3 discusses one source—the immigrants themselves—while Chapter 4 discusses another—local and national experts on immigration. Employing the Miami case study, techniques for accessing both groups and an analysis of the information obtained are provided.

NOTES

1. Many undocumented immigrants enter the country anticipating that, somewhere down the road, U.S. immigration policy will change and allow them to adjust their status (as the Immigration Reform and Control Act of 1986 did for thousands of undocumented immigrants).

2. Through personal communication with INS, Cuban refugee and adjustment year-of-entry statistics for the nation as a whole were obtained. The Miami portion of adjustments was calculated based on the proportion of all Cuban immigrants residing in Miami during these years (using census figures). The published immigration numbers were replaced with our year-of-arrival estimates for Cubans. Adjustments made up a much smaller proportion of immigrants from other countries during this period, and the assumption was made that entry statistics for other nationalities were not biased by adjustments. Therefore, the published INS number for arrivals adjusted with our calculation of Cuban entries is used as total legal immigration in a given year.

3. As noted in the following discussion, the designation of Miami in the pre-1983 data encompasses more than Miami proper. Most typically, reference is made to the Miami–Hialeah MSA.

4. Kenneth Hill provides a good overview of the difficulties of estimating undocumented aliens and describes the various estimation techniques that have been used in *Immigration Statistics: A Story of Neglect*, the National Academy of Sciences critique of immigration statistics, (1985).

5. The 1980–1985 estimates use Census Bureau estimates based on current population survey data (Woodrow, Passel, and Warren, 1987).

6. The census-derived estimates of undocumented immigration are acknowledged as undercounts; therefore, our estimates of undocumented aliens based on the census figures are conservative. The precise degree of downward bias is not known, but there is some evidence that the census estimate is a reasonably close, though conservative, estimate of those residing in the United States in 1980 (Warren and Passel, 1987). An independent survey in the Los Angeles area estimated that about 56 percent of the undocumented population had been counted in the 1980 census (Passel and Woodrow, 1987). This estimate corresponds to the estimate by Keely (1982) that between one-half and two-thirds of the undocumented population were included in the 1980 census.

7. These totals and percentages exclude any foreign-born naturalized citizens and, therefore, do not represent the entire immigrant population. The proportion of undocumented to documented aliens is used to calculate undocumented immigration (the UNDOC2 estimate) from 1972 forward. The procedure for estimating undocumented immigration makes the assumption that the proportion of undocumented

to documented immigrants remains steady from 1972 to 1988 for each of the regions and countries. Warren and Passel (1987) found some differences in the proportion of undocumented aliens during different entry periods.

The Warren and Passel proportions were developed, however, based on aliens residing in the United States during the 1980 census. These aliens may not reflect the actual entry proportions. Undocumented aliens may be less likely to remain in the United States for an extended period of time. If so, the proportion of undocumented aliens calculated from the 1980 population will underestimate the proportion of undocumented among aliens entering prior to 1980. The degree of underestimation will be greater for entrants during earlier years.

The problem of shifts in the proportion of undocumented aliens over time are alleviated, to some extent, because we are primarily interested in the relative year-to-year change in the numbers, rather then absolute totals. The problem will only be serious when there is a large, rapid change in the proportion of undocumented aliens. For example, the census-based estimation techniques will underestimate the recent influx of Central Americans, because it includes a higher proportion of undocumented aliens then earlier populations of Central American immigrants.

8. The school system refugee category includes immigrants who have applied for asylum as well as immigrants within the much narrower INS definition of the term. Refugees are included with undocumented because INS does not include them as documented immigrants until they adjust status.

9. The school-based estimate also assumes that undocumented aliens have the same proportion of school-age children as documented aliens and that these children enroll in school. If the undocumented population tends to include a lower proportion of children, and particularly a lower proportion of children in school, than the school-based estimate will underestimate immigration.

10. There is some evidence, at least for the Nicaraguan population, that foreign-born children are enrolled relatively quickly in the state school system. For the Nicaraguan students enrolling for the first time between September 18 and October 27, 1989, the average delay between entering the United States and enrolling in school was between ten and eleven months. About 50 percent of the Nicaraguan students registered within five months of their (self-reported) entry date, and about 80 percent were registered within a year of entry. On the other hand, about 13 percent waited more than two years to register, and a little less than 8 percent were registered more than three years after entry. Based on these statistics, there will be some lagged effect in school data, but effects beyond twelve months will be small.

11. Out-migration of the foreign-born population is expected to be a particularly important problem for the Cuban population because of the movement of Cubans (including women of child-bearing age) out of the case study county during the 1980s. Later, we examine this by holding Cubans out of some of the foreign-born population numbers.

12. The documentation of immigrants who were originally relocated to other areas of the nation and subsequently returned to Miami provides a host of problems. First, the communities which originally received these individuals had provided services and received revenues for a short duration of time. However, the determination of the exact figures cannot be discerned at this juncture in cross-sectional or longitudinal analyses.

Second, the timing of the original entrants and their eventual return to Miami presents another concern for determining immigration levels. For the purposes of this analysis, emigration between communities is suspected to be minimal, and off-set to some degree by the out-migration of other arriving immigrants.

13. The proportion of family classification immigrants adjusting status is generally lower then the proportion of new arrivals falling into this classification. This is particularly true for periods of high refugee influx, such as the early 1970s and 1980. Similarly, if a significant portion of the recent Central American immigrants adjust to immigrant status, the late 1980s adjustment data will show a relatively lower proportion of family classification immigrants than is currently tallied. But high refugee influxes aside, the proportion of family classification immigrants has increased sharply for both adjustment and new arrival immigrants.

CHAPTER 3 _____

Immigrant Decisions: Using a Field Survey

An examination of immigrant impacts would not be complete without considering the perceptions and attitudes of incoming documented and undocumented immigrants. To pursue informed policies, it is critical for managers to operate under assumptions that accurately reflect the attitudes, perceptions, and plans of all immigrants. A field survey provides a mechanism to gain such insights. Often, researchers focus on the mathematical techniques explained in Chapter 2 to extrapolate information without fully appreciating the nature of the population studied. Moreover, assuming that one immigrant group has similar demands and desires as another may lead to inaccurate and misleading findings.

A field survey can also compensate for one of the crucial weaknesses of the estimation techniques discussed in Chapter 2; their reduced reliability due to lagged status and relocation changes for the most recent years. To compensate for these limitations, the field interview is a necessary step in the process of determining impacts—both past, present, and, most enlightening, future. As a data gathering strategy, a field survey is a relatively inexpensive and uncomplicated process that can be repeated at regular intervals to provide updated information as deemed necessary.

The field survey allows the collection of primary data concerning immigrant decisions to migrate, their decisions on location once in the United States, and their work and migratory plans for the future. In addition, information on immigrant views of public services, as well as the sources of information immigrants use in developing perceptions, will allow managers to better anticipate future service requirements. The Miami case study offers examples of the collection and type of information which can be gathered directly from both legal and illegal immigrants.

FIELD SURVEY: METHODOLOGICAL ISSUES

Researchers have noted that strict adherence to survey research techniques is impossible, and often irrelevant, when studying populations that include a large component of undocumented immigrants. Stepick (1992) highlights four common problems: (1) enumerating the population in order to draw a sample; (2) constructing an interview instrument that considers cultural differences and remains reliable; (3) choosing appropriate interviewers; and (4) most important, finding cooperative respondents. Stepick further suggests that the methodological issues facing researchers can be overcome with appropriate techniques to accommodate various weaknesses associated with each research perspective.

Because of these methodological considerations, a multiphase opportunity sampling technique rather than traditional random selection is frequently utilized to select field survey participants, with special effort to include both legal and illegal immigrants (Stepick, 1992). A larger than normal sample of immigrants from available community sites is combined with a set of immigrants surveyed from randomly selected immigrant enclave households. The findings discussed here are based on 562 field survey interviews conducted with immigrants residing in South Florida. The thirteen-page interview instrument was developed in English and translated by native speakers into Spanish and Haitian Creole (see Appendix A for the questionnaire).

The questionnaire was developed to analyze two themes. One theme involved immigrant characteristics, attitudes, needs, behavior, and perceptions of government. Obviously, to plan for the impact of immigration, a manager needs to know as much as possible about the immigrant group. The second theme focused on the key decisions that immigrants must make in coming to the United States and the information sources utilized in making these decisions. The first theme illuminates the impact of past and future immigration to the United States, while the second concerns the viability of efforts to manage the flow of immigration.

Bilingual and trilingual interviewers were utilized to administer the surveys in one-on-one interviews. Interviews took from twenty to forty-five minutes to complete. The interviews were conducted in two phases. During the first phase, 362 immigrants were interviewed at community sites, including two offices of the INS and a number of churches, community-based organizations, and other community locations where immigrants congregate. Interviews were also conducted at a Miami sports arena which served as temporary shelter for Central American refugees during December 1988, and January 1989. The interview sites were identified by local community experts as locations where access to illegal immigrants would be good. The contact staff at the interview sites reported that the majority of respondents were currently illegal entrants or had initially entered the country as undocumented aliens.

The second phase of interviews was conducted to increase coverage of two targeted subpopulations, Nicaraguan and Haitian immigrants. Further, these interviews were used to validate the representativeness of the initial sample. This phase took trained interviewers into selected Haitian and Nicaraguan residential neighborhoods between June and October 1989. An additional 201 undocumented immigrants were surveyed in door-to-door interviews on random blocks. Samples from the two interview phases were combined for analysis after a detailed comparison revealed similar characteristics.[1]

CHARACTERISTICS OF FIELD SURVEY RESPONDENTS

In the Miami case study example, Nicaraguan and Haitian immigrants made up 81.7 percent of the overall sample (see Table 3.1). The distribution by nationality in the sample is not representative of the true proportions of established immigrants in Miami (see Chapter 2). While immigrants from Nicaragua and Haiti do represent the subgroups hypothesized to have the largest illegal contingent, their size was exaggerated by the over-sampling strategy to allow sufficient numbers for detailed analysis within each group.

This analysis permits an examination of cultural differences across immigrant groups and allows the targeting of policies to meet the special needs

Table 3.1
Immigrant Distribution by Reported Country of Birth

Country of Birth	Number	Percentage
Nicaraguan	237	42.2
Haiti	222	39.5
El Salvador	26	4.6
Guatemala	18	3.2
Cuba	17	3.0
Colombia	14	2.5
Honduras	7	1.3
Santo Domingo	4	0.7
Ecuador	4	0.7
Venezuela	4	0.7
Chile	2	0.4
Mexico	1	0.2
Panama	1	0.2
Uruguay	1	0.2
Costa Rica	1	0.2
Not Reported	3	0.5

of communities with large illegal immigrant populations. In subsequent analysis, the overall sample is examined and then comparisons are made across three subgroups: Haitians, Nicaraguans, and other Central Americans (including Salvadorans, Guatemalans, Mexicans, Panamanians, Costa Ricans, and Hondurans).[2]

Such an approach facilitates broad-based generalizations to be drawn where appropriate, such as language programs for a particular immigrant group. U.S. cities, especially coastal ones, tend to be multiethnic in their immigrant demographics, because factors that attract one immigrant group will likely attract a number of other immigrant groups (Simon, 1984). Therefore, the ability to delineate variations within the immigrant population is crucial.

With these considerations in mind, the survey findings show that the average (mean) time in the United States among the survey respondents is nearly four years (47 months). The distribution is skewed, with some respondents having resided in the United States for a number of years. A more accurate reflection of the average length of stay is the median value of two years (23.5 months). Roughly half of the undocumented immigrants have resided in the United States for two years or less. This value better reflects the actual enculturation period of the immigrants interviewed. Haitians interviewed had been in the United States the longest, then Nicaraguans, and then other Central Americans. More than half of the Nicaraguans in the sample had been in the United States less than two years, while only about 10 percent of the Haitians can be classified as recent arrivals.

Demographics: Age, Gender, Education, and Language

Immigrants in the sample were an average age of 33.5 years (see Table 3.2). The greatest concentration are between the ages of 27 and 37, with less than 2 percent over 65. Comparing across immigrant groups, Haitians in the sample were the oldest, with a mean age of 37, while Nicaraguans and other Central Americans were, on average, 31 years of age.[3]

Gender was evenly split in the sample: 52 percent of respondents were male and 48 percent were female. Within the three subgroups, the proportion of males to females varies somewhat, with a high of 57.6 percent male for Nicaraguans to a low of 37 percent male for the Central Americans. These figures suggest a higher proportion of females in the largely undocumented population, rebutting the typical picture of an undocumented immigrant as a young male. The proportion of males among immigrants arriving within the last two years is not significantly different from the proportion of males in the rest of the sample.

The median years of education for immigrants interviewed is 9 years. A little under 10 percent of the participants had 5 or less years of education, with a small percent indicating they had never attended school. Haitians

Table 3.2
Immigrant Demographic Profile

	Total	Nicaraguans	Haitians	Central Americans
Average Age	33.5	31.2	36.9	30.8
Percentage Over 65	1.4	1.7	1.5	0.0
Median Education in Years	9.0	9.0	8.0	9.0
Proportion Male	52.0	57.6	54.1	37.0
Average Months in United States	46.0	18.8	88.2	9.6
Median	23.5	10.0	84.0	4.0
Median Current Savings	0.0	0.0	0.0	0.0
Median Weekly Income	0.0	0.0	118.0	0.0
Percentage Who:				
Speak English	23.7	11.9	40.0	15.1
Read English	18.5	13.6	25.5	17.0
Write English	16.3	10.6	23.2	13.2
Percentage Who: Write in Native Tongue	–	98.7	42.0	98.1
Read in Native Tongue	–	98.7	51.1	98.1

had the least education, with 7.95 average years of schooling, and nearly one-fifth of the Haitian sample indicated they had not completed 1 year of schooling.[4] Nicaraguans averaged 9.45 years of education, and Central Americans averaged 9.13 years.[5]

English proficiency and literacy was rare among respondents. Only 23.7 percent of the aliens indicated they could speak English, and fewer reported reading or writing English. Not surprising, the ability to speak English (and to a lesser extent, read and write English) appears to be a function of the length of time an immigrant has resided in the United States. Only 13.5 percent of recent immigrants (those who have been in the United States two years or less) indicated a proficiency in English, compared to 23.7 percent in the sample as a whole.[6] Respondents were also asked about their ability to read and write in their native tongue. About 42 percent of the Haitian respondents indicated they could write in their native tongue and 51 percent indicated they could read. A much higher percentage (98%) of the Nicaraguans and Central Americans indicated they could write in their native tongue, and about the same number reported the ability to read. In both cases, the reported literacy rate among immigrants is higher than the overall literacy rate of their home country (23% in Haiti and 88% in Nicaragua).

Based on the survey respondents' stated occupations (Table 3.3), and combining the categories of student, none/unemployed, and housewife, over 30 percent of this immigrant group is not a part of the workforce. The

Table 3.3
Occupational Profile: Percentage Reported in Each Category

	All	Haitian	Nicaraguan	Central Americans
Student	19.5 (56)	24.1 (7)	21.3 (37)	8.5 (4)
None/Unemployed	12.2 (35)	13.8 (4)	14.4 (25)	6.4 (3)
Professional	15.7 (45)	17.2 (5)	14.9 (26)	12.8 (6)
Craft	11.8 (34)	10.3 (3)	8.0 (14)	25.5 (12)
Domestic Service	11.1 (32)	3.4 (1)	12.1 (21)	14.9 (7)
Sales	4.9 (14)	6.9 (2)	4.6 (8)	4.3 (2)
Clerk	8.0 (23)	3.4 (1)	10.9 (19)	4.3 (2)
Skilled	5.9 (17)	10.3 (3)	5.2 (9)	8.5 (4)
Farm Work	4.2 (12)	3.4 (1)	4.6 (8)	4.3 (2)
Self-Employed	1.4 (4)	3.4 (1)	0.6 (1)	2.1 (1)
Laborer	2.4 (7)	3.4 (1)	1.1 (2)	8.5 (4)
Service	2.4 (7)		1.7 (3)	
Housewife	0.3 (1)		0.6 (1)	

Note: Actual number in parentheses; respondents in United States two years or less.

remaining immigrants show a wide range of skill levels. The percentage of trained or skilled occupation respondents contradicts current literature in this area and the INS data on documented immigrants (see Chapter 2). The occupation indicated, however, does not necessarily represent current employment in that field (and the average weekly income reported suggests that very few of the immigrants are employed in their reported occupation). There are very few immigrants in the sample who characterized themselves as housewives. It suggests that virtually all of the immigrants would like (or feel compelled) to work outside of the home. The immigrants in the sample, like undocumented immigrants in other studies, have a very high labor force participation rate, when they can find jobs.

The occupational distribution of more recent immigrants differs in several respects from immigrants who have been in the United States for more than two years. Among the long-term immigrants there were fewer students, a higher incidence of unemployment (across all nationalities), fewer professionals, more self-employment, and more immigrants involved in sales-related jobs. The pattern suggests a larger number of long-term immigrants fall within the informal sector of the economy and are employed in low-level, marginal jobs. However, the difference may be primarily perceptual. Newly arriving immigrants likely see themselves either in the same role they held in their prior country or in the role they would like to hold in this country. Over time, the economic and social realities of immigration and, quite likely, questionable legal status intrude, and the immigrant adjusts his or her perception to actual occupational opportunities.

The below poverty level condition of these immigrants is reflected in the amount of current savings and weekly family income (as reported in Table 3.2).

The respondents reported a mean level of current savings of $637, and a mean weekly family income of $119. These values understate the poverty of many of the immigrants, because a few immigrants reported high current savings (up to $60,000) and/or high weekly incomes. The median level of both reported savings and family weekly income was zero. In other words, more than half the respondents reported having no savings or weekly income.

Haitians in the sample appear to be in a slightly better financial position than other groups, as reflected in the mean of $770 for current savings (median of zero) and a mean weekly income in the United States of $194 (median of $118). The better position of the Haitians may be entirely due to their longer tenure in the United States. Not surprising, there are significant correlations between length of time in the United States and family weekly income ($r = 0.47$, significant at 0.000) reported by the immigrants. Over time, the immigrants manage to increase their income. In multivariate analysis, the length of stay indicator is the primary determinant of income and savings, and once length of stay is controlled, Haitians actually make less per week and have lower current savings than other groups in the sample.

The aggregate picture of the immigrant participating in this survey indicates an impoverished, poorly educated, non-English-speaking population. While they possess a wide range of skill levels, the inability to speak English limits their opportunities and places them in competition with the marginal native resident. Earlier research on immigration reports similar immigration patterns in prior years. Portes and Stepick (1985), for instance, found that later waves of Cuban and Haitian immigrants were comprised of more disadvantaged individuals than their respective pre-established immigrant communities.

Last, learning English is a reported priority for immigrants. About 71 percent of those surveyed who do not know English intend to study English. However, these plans may never come to fruition. The literature in this area argues that learning English becomes secondary to vocational skill development upon realization that non-English-speaking immigrants can function and prosper if there is an established economic enclave representing their particular ethnic group. The number of non-English-speaking aliens can be expected to have significant effects on local government. The political processes of debate, negotiation, and compromise become much more complex. This is evidenced in local South Florida jurisdictions, where official translators are required for political meetings, including city commission proceedings.

Municipal administration also becomes increasingly complex and frustrating as the importance of bilingual and trilingual employees is magnified. Foreign language skills become a criteria for government and nonprofit agency employment, potentially leading to perceived discrimination against native-born citizens. The frustration level of both citizens and administrators is likely to rise and their satisfaction fall when language mismatches occur. In short, when language barriers exist, service delivery becomes far more complex, more expensive, and more likely to fall short of expectations.

IMMIGRANT ATTITUDES AND DECISIONS

One specific use of a field survey is to assemble a profile of the decision process undergone prior to immigrating. People migrate between nations for a host of reasons, and there are a number of theories used to understand the immigration phenomena. The theory that has received the most attention by scholars (and is broad enough to encompass many of the more specific theories) is the "push–pull" theory of international migration. The theory proposes that migration is greatly influenced by economic and political conditions in the sending and receiving countries, resulting in a set of push–pull factors (Briggs, 1984). Adverse economic or political conditions in the sending country "push" immigrants to leave. They are then "pulled" to the receiving country as a result of the more favorable conditions, whether economic, political, or environmental (Yarnold, 1990).

Early in U.S. history, most immigrants came to this country to escape adverse conditions in their host countries, such as war, famine, and unemployment (U.S. Immigration and Naturalization Service, 1991).[7] As a result of these factors, immigrants were pushed out of their respective countries. The idea of inexpensive, undeveloped farmlands and the potential for employment pulled most immigrants to the United States rather than other developing countries.

A specific example of this process is the potato famine experienced in Ireland during the 1840s and early 1850s. The famine forced many Irish farmers and residents to leave their homes, lands, and country. The Western land rush and other opportunities caused them to seek refuge in the United States. These push–pull factors resulted in 1.8 million Irish immigrants landing on the shores of the United States during this period. During the same time frame, Germany was facing severe economic depression and rapid political turmoil, leading 1.2 million Germans to migrate to the United States.

In fact, every historical wave of immigration to the United States can be evaluated based on the concept of push–pull. In spite of its popularity, however, this theory does have limitations. One of the major limitations of the push–pull theory is that, as an aggregate, macro-level theory, it does not capture nor explain variations in individual decisions to migrate. That is, if economic reasons are the primary causes for migration, then why do not all individuals in the same economic circumstances in the sending nation migrate? Further, the theory does not incorporate the criteria immigrants use to determine whether or not legal channels should be pursued prior to migrating.

With these issues in mind, a better understanding of why people migrate and, once a decision is made to migrate, why they choose to reside in a particular host community, is important for local administrators. At this juncture, it is important to understand that individual reasons for migrating may not always converge with the push–pull theory used to understand international migration. For local governments and the services they provide, a crucial issue involves the preparations made by immigrants in anticipation of immigrating to the United States. Better prepared immigrants who have specific plans upon arrival will have a different (although not necessarily smaller) impact on local government after arrival. It is likely that they will have less immediate impact, but may more quickly become aware of services that are available and therefore have a greater impact than unprepared immigrants over time. Or, at a minimum, utilize services such as education, parks and recreation, and healthcare at a much quicker pace. Results of the Miami field survey indicate that a majority of participants made few or no plans for emigrating from their country. Of the 562 respondents, less than 15 percent reported a specific amount of money saved prior to immigration. When queried regarding other plans made in anticipation of coming to the United States, the majority (90%) responded negatively to saving household goods or clothing.[8] Of those who had made plans, 15 percent indicated they had learned English, and 4 percent reported learning a job skill. Although only 1 percent contacted potential employers, 3 percent had jobs waiting for them on their arrival. About 20 percent of those interviewed had contacted relatives in the United States, and an additional 10 percent had contacted friends in the United States prior to leaving their country. In sum, the immigrants surveyed arrived with little or no financial resources and with no clear plans for employment, housing, or other basic necessities for self-sufficiency.

The Immigrant's Decision to Emigrate

Respondents were also asked what sources and how much information they received prior to immigrating about life in the United States. That is, what was the source of their nearly universal, positive expectations about life in the United States.[9] Of those interviewed, 44 percent stated that the primary reason for leaving their country was the desire for political asylum. Whether this was a coached response to INS criteria for entry cannot be determined by the current analysis. Other primary reasons cited were poverty or economic conditions, opportunities available in the United States, education, and relatives in the United States. A higher proportion of Haitian immigrants, however, indicated economic reasons for their decision to emigrate.

Family and friends in the home country contributed most of the information about life in the United States available to respondents (see Table 3.4). It is interesting to note that the immigrants interviewed had received little information about life in the United States from family and friends living in the United States.[10]

Table 3.4
Importance of Various Information Sources in Deciding to Immigrate

	All	Nicaraguan	Haitian	Central Americans
Family in U.S.	2.2	2.0	2.6	1.4
Friends in U.S.	2.3	2.5	2.7	2.2
Family in Prior Country	3.4	3.9	2.5	4.2
Friends in Prior Country	3.3	3.7	2.6	4.1
U.S. Government	1.1	1.1	1.1	1.1
Prior Government	1.1	1.1	1.0	1.3
U.S. Newspapers	1.2	1.1	1.1	1.4
U.S. Radio	1.2	1.1	1.1	1.4
U.S. Television	1.2	1.1	1.1	1.5
Prior Newspapers	1.2	1.3	1.1	1.3
Prior Radio	1.3	1.3	1.3	1.3
Prior Television	1.2	1.2	1.2	1.3
Self from Visits	1.1	1.1	1.2	1.1
Church	1.3	1.4	1.3	1.3
Percentage Who Had Visited U.S. Prior to Immigrating	14	9	21	3.7

Note: Average scores reported based on 5-unit scale derived from the following question: "I'm going to read you a list of people and places where you could have gotten information which helped you decide to immigrate. Please tell me approximately how much information you got from each source: 'All,' 'Most,' 'Some,' 'Just a Little,' or 'None.'" "All" was scored a 5, and "none" was scored a 1.

Other traditional sources of information about life in the United States were insignificant (e.g., government, media, and church). Institutional avenues do not emerge as significant information channels in the formation of the immigrant's view of life in the United States. At the low end of the scale, information received from the U.S. and home-country governments, U.S. and home-country media, and the church was negligible for all groups.

Findings related to respondents' sources of information regarding their decision to immigrate were similar. Hence, traditional government sources and channels appear to have had little impact on immigration decisions. Either they have not been used or they have little impact when used. Field survey findings cast doubt on their efficacy as a means of influencing immigration. Therefore, policies and mechanisms that tap into the informal social network of family and friends and use identified opinion leaders within the home country are likely to be more effective than official channels.[11]

The Immigrant's Decision Regarding Residency in the United States

After arriving in the United States, the immediate impact on local governments is determined by the immigrant's initial decision on residence. As shown in Table 3.5, information from family and friends in the home country had the greatest effect on where the immigrants located. Haitians, however, did not rely as heavily on these sources of information, and were more likely to rely on information from family and friends who had preceded them to the United States. As with the previous issues, information received from the U.S. and home-country governments, U.S. and home-country media, and religious organizations was negligible. Social network information obtained in the immigrant's prior country remains dominant. The emerging theme is that immigrants rely almost exclusively on information sources inside personal social networks in their previous countries. Relatively few access information from the United States prior to their arrival, even from friends or family that have preceded them.

In determining specifically where to live, many immigrants were unable to specify a primary reason. Among those who could cite a reason, cost, availability, and location are the most common. However, housing decisions do not appear to be made through a formal decision process. Apparently, immigrants either learn of established immigrant communities in the United States based on information from friends and family in their prior country, or drift to them without considering alternatives. For municipalities, this means that once established, immigrant enclaves will attract subsequent newcomers.

Table 3.5
Importance of Various Information Sources Regarding Where to Live Once in the United States

	All	Nicaraguan	Haitian	Central Americans
Family in U.S.	2.2	2.0	2.8	1.6
Friends in U.S.	2.6	2.7	2.5	2.5
Family in Prior Country	3.2	3.7	2.1	4.1
Friends in Prior Country	2.9	3.3	2.1	3.9
U.S. Government	1.2	1.2	1.1	1.9
Prior Government	1.0	1.1	1.0	1.0
U.S. Newspapers	1.2	1.2	1.3	1.4
U.S. Radio	1.2	1.2	1.1	1.4
U.S. Television	1.2	1.2	1.1	1.3
Prior Newspapers	1.2	1.2	1.0	1.2
Prior Radio	1.2	1.2	1.2	1.3
Prior Television	1.1	1.1	1.1	1.2
Self from Visits	1.1	1.1	1.2	1.0
Church	1.2	1.3	1.3	1.2

Note: Average scores reported based on 5-unit scale derived from the following question: "How much information did you get from each of the following about where to live in the United States: 'All,' 'Most,' 'Some,' 'Just a Little,' or 'None'?" "All" was scored a 5, and "none" was scored a 1.

Immigrant Plans for the Next Five Years

To project future demands and impacts on municipal services, all interviewees were asked their plans for the next five years. The results are reported in Table 3.6. As shown, about six out of every ten immigrants plan to bring more family; about half of the Haitians, 60 percent of the Nicaraguans, and 75 percent of the Central Americans indicated this personal goal.

All groups indicate an interest in furthering their education and learning new job skills. Most immigrants were not looking to change jobs at the time of the interview. The cross-nationality differences were supported in multivariate analysis and were, in fact, strengthened when length of stay, education, and age were controlled. In general, the younger and more recent the immigrant, the more likely an interest in further education and learning new job skills was present.

The majority of respondents showed an interest in learning English, the lowest proportion being among Haitians. When looking only at immigrants who have no prior knowledge of English, the percentage planning to learn English is even larger. The strongest determinant of plans to learn English is length of time in the United States. The longer the immigrant is in the United States, the less interest the immigrant has in improving English skills, even when that immigrant indicates no English abilities. Perhaps the immigrants who have been in the United States longer have learned that English is not essential or that English is harder to learn than initially thought. In either case, plans of recent immigrants to learn English may, for many, never come to fruition.

Table 3.6
Immigrant Plans for the Future: Percentage Indicating Selected Plans for the Next Five Years

	All	Nicaraguan	Haitian	Central Americans
Bring More Family to to the U.S.	60.0	62.7	52.5	75.9
Go to School	55.7	52.1	61.4	40.7
Learn New Job Skill	52.1	49.6	49.1	66.7
Change Jobs	28.4	18.5	41.8	20.4
Become a U.S. Citizen	54.3	57.9	35.2	90.7
Learn English	71.1	79.8	60.6	75.5
Learn English (no prior English knowledge)	80.2	85.9	67.2	88.9
Remain in Dade County	64.4	60.8	70.8	56.3

About half of the respondents plan to become citizens. However, far fewer Haitians have citizenship plans then either Nicaraguans or Central Americans. This in large part represents a measure of acculturation due to longevity. The Haitians have been here long enough to realize that obtaining citizenship is a long and difficult process. In multivariate analysis, the length of time the immigrant has been in the United States is the most important determinant of citizenship plans. Immigrants who have been in the United States longer are much less likely to plan on becoming citizens over the next five years. Last, as a measure of their mobility, respondents were questioned about their plans regarding relocation. Overall, a majority indicated they planned to stay in the local area for an indefinite period.

In sum, the immigrants surveyed are not what is termed in the immigration literature, *sojourners*—people interested in finding temporary work and then returning to their country. Instead, they tend to be true immigrants with plans for settling permanently in the community as the first arrivals of nuclear and extended families. These immigrants may best be perceived as "advance family scouts." In particular, more recent immigrants are often the first arrivals and come with plans to bring additional family members to the United States once they have established themselves.

Immigrant plans reflect a long-term goal of enculturation, in that they desire to become citizens, learn English, raise families, and pursue new lines of work. The case study shows how immigrants clearly wish upon arrival to become Americanized. As time passes, however, this early goal becomes less important or realistic. Municipalities faced with such immigrants will therefore need long-term plans and policies, and will find short-term contingency measures inadequate.

Immigrant Attitudes toward and Utilization of Government Services

While the characteristics of immigrants, as well as their numbers, lead to the expectation that additional government services would be required, the immigrants surveyed do not exhibit a strong history of utilizing government services. Less than 5 percent of the respondents indicate that they have approached the U.S. government about a problem, and even less have approached governments in their prior county. Their resistance to contact government may reflect a fear of government in general, or a low expectation of what services government can provide. Roughly 22 percent of the immigrants surveyed felt that government officials considered the opinions of citizens. This feeling existed across all ethnic groups. There was even less faith in government's consideration of citizens' opinions among longer-term immigrants (controlling for nationality, age, and education).[12] In addition, longer-term immigrants indicated less contact with government.

A second measure of the propensity to use government services is gathered from immigrants' sources of help when facing problems like illness, homelessness, unemployment, and crime. The immigrants indicate varying utilization of support networks (friends, family, neighbors, coworkers, etc.), professional resources (lawyers, doctors, etc.), government (police, firemen, etc.), and the media (see Table 3.7).

In multivariate analysis with controls for nationality, education, and age, the longer the immigrant resided in the United States, the higher the immigrant's overall reliance on self and government, and the lower the reliance on a social network. Increased dependency on government had the strongest relationship with length of stay. Longer tenure in the United States was also associated with a decrease in the number of immigrants who are not sure where to go for particular problems. In sum, over time immigrants appear to rely more on formal agencies and less on informal personal networks. For city managers, this means that recent immigrants will make less direct demands on services but over time their demands will increase, which may or may not bode well for original host communities.

Last, in terms of a general overall attitude toward the perceived need for government services, a general index variable was developed. For this index, a score of 5 indicates a higher general perceived need for increased government services and a score of 1 indicates a lower general perceived need. As a total group, the immigrants agreed on the need for increased government services.

Table 3.7
Perceived Source of Help for Various Problems (Percentage)

Problem	Self	Social Network	Professional	Government	Media	Unsure
Sick	6.8	43.2	43.1	0.7	0.0	1.4
Need Home	11.4	68.9	0.9	4.4	7.3	6.2
Need ride to Hosp.	8.2	73.8	2.5	4.8	0.0	7.8
Quest. about law	1.8	7.7	77.2	6.9	0.4	5.0
Quest. about rights	2.1	5.9	79.0	7.7	0.2	3.9
Need Job	11.7	36.5	2.1	8.4	31.5	6.8
Need Food	8.5	72.1	1.4	9.3	0.0	5.7
Unfair treatment	39.0	21.4	21.0	12.3	0.2	5.3
No Running Water	3.9	8.5	70.5	13.5	0.0	2.7
Fight w/ Neighbor	38.3	10.5	9.3	34.7	0.7	5.2
Need Trash Removed	10.7	5.3	16.9	47.5	0.5	14.4
Have Fire	2.3	10.1	9.3	68.7	0.0	7.1
Robbed	11.6	6.6	0.9	76.2	0.0	4.8
Assaulted	4.1	5.5	3.2	82.7	0.0	4.1

Note: Average scores reported based on 5-unit scale derived from the following question: "How much information did you get from each of the following about where to live in the United States? Please tell me approximately how much information you got from each source: 'All,' 'Most,' 'Some,' 'Just a Little,' or 'None.'" "All" was scored a 5, and "none" was scored a 1.

The social services, particularly programs for the elderly and youths, were ranked at the top of the list for all immigrant groups. Improved bus service, parks, medical care, and garbage collection fell in the middle of the priority list for the average immigrant, but the precise ordering varied by immigrant group. The Haitians ranked medical care highest among the middle-range services and then parks, buses, and garbage collection. The Nicaraguans and Central Americans gave bus services the highest priority among the second-tier services and then parks, garbage, and, finally, medical care. The criminal justice services were given the lowest priority by the total sample respondents and by all of the sample subgroups except Nicaraguans, who ranked police services fourth overall.

These findings raise the question of whether differences in perceived need for services is a function of cultural differences or length of stay in the United States. If the latter is true, municipalities may experience an increasing demand for services over time as immigrant groups become enculturated, regardless of the immigrant group being analyzed. To test this question, the relationship between length of time in the United States and immigrant group attitude was examined.

Table 3.8 examines the effect that length of time spent in the United States has on selected opinions. Again, the relationship of these variables varies across groups. Noting that a positive correlation reflects an attitude of increased need for government services over time, groups tend to increase their perceptions of service needs over time. In multivariate analysis examining the impact of length of stay, nationality, age, and education on the demand for various services, length of stay was the strongest independent predictor of support for every policy area identified in the survey: elderly programs, parks, youth programs, medical care, prisons, garbage collection, bus service, courts, and police.

SUMMARY

The case study field survey reveals the importance of immigrant-specific information. Attitudes, abilities, and expectations of immigrants were found to vary across groups and importantly by the length of time each had spent in the United States. Policy making and municipal management without immigrant subgroup knowledge is a recipe for failure.

The field interviews provided a wide range of information useful to public administrators. For example, the median of both savings and weekly income reported by field survey respondents was zero dollars. In addition, a large proportion of respondents fall into the informal sector of the economy, having low-level, marginal jobs. However, virtually all respondents wanted to be employed in a job outside of their home. Over time, the immigrants managed to increase their incomes and acquire modest savings, but not to the point of satisfaction with their economic situations. Surprisingly, even

Table 3.8
Correlations and Significance of Length of Time in the United States with Attitude toward Government and Economy Scales and Perceived Need for Selected Programs (Level of Significance)

	All	Nicaraguan	Haitian	Central Americans
Need for Government				
Services	.48	.56	.19	.48
	(.00)	(.00)	(.01)	(.00)
Satisfaction with:				
the Economy	-.20	-.19	-.08	.00
	(.00)	(.00)	(.22)	(.98)
Government Responsiveness	-.06	.29	-.07	.03
	(.19)	(.00)	(.34)	(.86)
More Youth Programs	.43	.60	.18	.36
	(.00)	(.00)	(.01)	(.00)
More Parks	.34	.40	.06	.29
	(.00)	(.02)	(.39)	(.03)
More Elderly Programs	.18	.33	.08	-.08
	(.00)	(.00)	(.27)	(.59)
Better Garbage Collection	.36	.33	.18	.42
	(.00)	(.00)	(.01)	(.00)
More Police	.16	.47	-.02	.17
	(.00)	(.00)	(.75)	(.22)
More Courts	.27	.24	.23	.18
	(.00)	(.00)	(.00)	(.21)
More Prisons	.27	.24	.07	.44
	(.00)	(.00)	(.33)	(.00)
More Buses	.32	.52	.15	.41
	(.00)	(.00)	(.03)	(.00)
More Medical Care	.47	.44	.04	.53
	(.00)	(.00)	(.57)	(.00)

though the immigrants in the survey would seem to require extensive government assistance, particularly social services, the respondents did not indicate a high demand for such services. Few had approached the government for help.

Regarding their plans prior to immigration, respondents made few or no preparations prior to immigrating. Immigrants, therefore, generally arrive with little or no financial resources and with no clear plans for employment, housing, or other necessities. Exacerbating this lack of planning, immigrants, particularly recent arrivals, rely almost exclusively on information sources inside their personal social networks in their prior countries. The significance of these findings is the inability of government entities to easily influence immigrant decisions.

The future plans of immigrants also have implications for municipalities and their administrators. About 60 percent of the respondents plan to bring additional family into the United States within five years. A higher proportion of the most recent immigrants plan on bringing additional family members to the United States in the future. While a majority of immigrants plan on learning English, the longer they reside in the United States, the less likely they are to learn English.

Length of stay is the strongest predictor of demand for improved government services. The longer the respondent has been in the United States, the more the respondent agrees that government services should be improved. This held true for all immigrants and every municipal service measured in the study: elderly programs, parks, youth programs, medical care, prisons, garbage collection, bus service, courts, and police. Over time, immigrants developed less faith in government's consideration of citizens' opinions, had less contact with government, and became more cynical about government and public officials.

Immigrants of all nationalities have shared characteristics of avoiding formal and official information sources and of gravitating toward established enclaves once in the United States. They also share an initial desire to become citizens and enculturate. However, they differ significantly by nationality in terms of the skills and resources they bring to this country and the services and demands they will likely put upon local governments. Reflecting cultures and conditions in their home countries, some arrive ill prepared to succeed and survive. However, immigrant groups that are the least prepared and apparently the most in need of services, are precisely those that are least likely to make direct demands on municipal services. Nevertheless, their presence will be felt indirectly through medical care, schools, and housing, and eventually upon municipal revenues and expenditures.

In addition to the field survey, there is another rich source of information concerning immigration and service use by immigrants that can be collected with relative ease and at low cost. Local and national experts can be tapped via a mailed survey technique known as a Delphi Survey, the focus of Chapter 4.

NOTES

1. The samples were broken down by nationality, and the Haitian and Nicaraguan components of each were compared. The within-subgroups examination showed similarity on a variety of characteristics including age, years of education, gender, the number of immigrants who brought family with them to the United States, and certain plans for the future.

2. The remaining group was considered too small and too diverse to analyze as a separate set.

3. It must be emphasized that the demographics presented are those of the sample. In many respects, the sample is not representative of the total immigrant population in the city. As noted, this study focuses on selected nationalities and more recent immigrants. Moreover, the interviews were conducted with adults and, in the first phase, in settings with a potentially higher proportion of families then may be typical among other immigrant groups.

4. Recent Haitian immigrants, about 10 percent of all Haitians in the sample, report more education (median education level of ten years) than Haitians that have been here longer (median education level of seven years).

5. The recent Nicaraguan arrivals in the sample have slightly less education (median level of nine years) than Nicaraguans who have been in the United States at least two years (median of ten years of education). The other Central American group has too few respondents to make meaningful comparisons based on time of arrival.

6. In part, the difference across nationality is a function of length of stay in the United States. The Haitians in the sample had, on average, been in the United States for seventy-six months, while the Nicaraguans had been in the United States for an average of twenty months and other Central Americans for an average of ten months. In multivariate analysis, months in the United States (logged) was the primary determinant of the ability to speak English. But even when controlling for length of stay, a higher proportion of Haitians speak English then Nicaraguans or other Central Americans. There is, however, no difference in the ability to read or write English across nationalities once length of stay is controlled.

7. Other factors played an important role in migrating, such as family reunification, deportation and exile from the sending nation, and religious freedom, but escape provides the major justification for the mass migration experienced during this period (Jones, 1960).

8. A larger proportion of Haitian respondents (22%) indicated they saved household goods in preparation for emigration than either Nicaraguan or Central American respondents (less than 3%). This probably reflects the different demands of emigration by boat.

9. In terms of what they expect life to be like in the United States prior to immigrating, all groups are similar in their expectations. They anticipate living conditions, job opportunities, wages, government services, police protection, access to material goods, political freedom, healthcare, education, opportunities for their children, food, amenities, and personal safety to be better here than in their home country. Only in crime did the United States rate worse than their prior countries with a substantial number of immigrants. In all other areas, the immigrants felt and expected conditions and opportunities here to be superior.

10. The three subgroups tended to rely about the same on information from family and friends in the United States (Haitians with means of 2.7 and 2.3; Nicaraguans, 2.6 and 2.8; and other Central Americans, 1.3 and 2.4). The Nicaraguans and other Central Americans were slightly more likely to receive information from friends in the United States than family in the United States. Although the differences in the amount of information received from family and friends are small, they suggest (especially for the Central American sample) that the persons interviewed in this study may be the first members of their families to come to the United States.

Family and friends in the United States were more important in the formulation of the immigrants' views of the United States for the Nicaraguans in the sample who have been in the United States for some length of time. There is a relatively strong and statistically significant correlation between months in the United States (logged) and information from family in the United States ($r = 0.42$, sign. < 0.001), information from friends in the United States ($r = 0.33$, sign. < 0.001), and visits to the United States prior to immigration ($r = 0.21$, sign. < 0.001). There is a negative correlation between logged months in the United States and information from family in prior country (r = –0.30, sign. < 0.001) and information from friends in prior country (r = –0.17, sign. < 0.001). The recent immigrants from Nicaragua clearly have less contact with friends and family in the United States prior to immigration and are likely to have less support from these sources when they arrive.

11. These findings may be skewed to some degree, since respondents represent only individuals who have migrated. There is no attempt to understand why individuals did not migrate. For nonmigrating individuals, government sources may or may not be significant.

12. More educated immigrants tended to feel better about government's consideration of citizens' opinions.

CHAPTER 4

Using the Experts: A Delphi Survey

To plan for immigration needs, local managers need some comprehension of potential future immigration flows. Many factors that impact the migration of individuals across nation-states are beyond the control of the receiving nation. However, at the local level, many problems can be anticipated and ameliorated to some degree through information and forecasting. A Delphi survey of designated national and local experts is one useful technique for the collection of information useful for planning.

The Delphi technique utilized in this case study employed interviews with immigration experts to assess projections of potential future immigration and the likely impact of future immigrants on government services. The primary purpose of the Delphi technique is to generate consensus among "experts" in the field regarding the phenomenon under investigation. The instability of immigration trends makes the Delphi approach more useful than purely statistical estimations. The technique also allows the consideration of specific questions (in this case, relating to immigration s effects on revenue and service delivery) as well as interactions among the effects which cannot be discerned by statistical methods. The Delphi process is used to structure expert opinion in predicting potential impacts developed through a consensus gathering process.

The Delphi technique employed in this case study began with the formulation of initial instruments and the identification of two groups of experts (national and local) through the use of a modified snowball sampling procedure. After initial responses were collected and analyzed, a second-round instrument was developed and sent to the respondents seeking explication of initial findings.

Two distinct groups were utilized to collect the information. The first group consisted of a national sample of experts on immigration flow and international political trends. Their role was to identify potential shifts in the influx of immigrants as well as the likelihood of these shifts.[1] The second group of experts included a sample of local government officials and nongovernment service providers able to identify likely current impacts based on their more specific, local experiences. Combining local and national experts allows managers to incorporate information about potential national trends, and also to anticipate local issues that experts having a purely national perspective may not be familiar with.

The first questionnaire was designed to identify broad trends and impacts (see Appendix B). The questions were open-ended, requiring the experts to discuss broad trends and issues relevant to studying immigrant impacts. The first iteration of both Delphi instruments was mailed to over 400 national and local experts, with a 16 percent return rate.[2] From the first iteration, twenty national and forty-four local members of the original expert groups were identified and indicated that they would participate in a second wave.[3] The national group included academics, politicians, and federal administrators. The local group included a lawyer, a U.S. attorney, a politician, a local representative of the Immigration and Naturalization Service, nine representatives of immigrant organizations or nongovernment service providers, and nine high-level local administrators, including three representatives of police departments, two officials in fire or fire rescue organizations, two general government administrators, a planner, and a representative of a department of economic development. Six local respondents did not indicate their organizational affiliation.

The second-round questionnaires (see Appendix C) elicited predictions regarding the level of immigration from various countries as well as the percentage of immigrants from each country possessing specific characteristics, such as the age and proportion of skilled laborers. Last, experts were asked to rank-order immigration impact on specified municipal services.

DELPHI RESULTS: FORECASTING IMMIGRATION

As an introduction to examining the experts predictions regarding future immigration, the hesitancy of both expert groups to provide long-term projections must be noted. This indicates that the nature of forecasting immigration is more an "art" than a "science." National experts realize forecasting immigration is a risky business and were reluctant to make such projections. Local experts were, however, more open to making projections than the national experts. We hypothesize that local experts have either detailed knowledge of their communities and their immigrant mix (of which national experts may not be cognizant) or local experts have not been exposed to the public nature and scrutiny of their estimates. In either case, local experts were more amiable to providing future immigration flows than national experts.

During the initial iteration of the Delphi survey conducted in 1988, experts were asked to identify the countries and regions of the world where a majority of immigration to the Miami area would originate. These "target" countries were isolated in order to provide a benchmark for analyzing future projections. If current immigration policy is to be maintained (where preference is given to family reunification), then projections should account for this potentiality. In addition, analysts should be aware of the changing nature of immigration policy and develop alternative scenarios to capture these probabilities.

Expert Projections

Both national and local experts were asked in the second round to project the number of immigrants they expected to arrive and settle in the United States and the City of Miami during 1989 and between 1990 and 2000.[4] Obtaining 1989 projections facilitated comparison with actual 1989 reported immigration figures, and thereby allowed an evaluation of the validity of Delphi forecasts in this area (see Chapter 6 for discussion). Local experts were asked for 1989 and 1990–2000 total projections and to indicate the percentage of these immigrants arriving from each of the six target countries identified in the first round (Cuba, Haiti, Nicaragua, Guatemala, El Salvador, and Honduras).[5] In the course of analysis, the percentage responses were combined with the estimates of overall immigration to develop immigration projections for each of the target countries.

The local experts projected (based on a median response) that 35,260 immigrants would arrive in Miami in 1989 and that 400,000 immigrants would arrive between 1990 and 2000 (Table 4.1). The largest proportion were expected to be from Nicaragua, followed by Cuba, Haiti, and other Central American countries. The local experts do not expect a major change in the mix of nationalities from 1989 to 2000. The relative percentages were basically the same for both time periods, although a somewhat larger proportion of immigrants were expected to come from El Salvador during the 1990–2000 period.

More detailed projections were obtained from the national experts. They were asked to provide 1989 and 1990–2000 minimum, maximum, and most likely projections for each of the target countries. Despite an effort in the second round to restrict the panel to national experts familiar with South Florida and the City of Miami specifically, some experts indicated they could not provide the requested projections. This illustrates one of the difficulties in using the Delphi technique. Although the instability of trends and difficulty of projection makes the Delphi approach more useful than statistical projections, there is often a reluctance on behalf of experts to make future projections.

Nevertheless, the projections generated by national experts were quite similar to those provided by local experts. The total for the "most likely"

Table 4.1
Immigration Projections: Local Experts

Nationality	1989			1990–2000		
	Low	High	Standard Deviation	Low	High	Standard Deviation
Cuban	1,250	80,000	16.9	15,000	250,000	84.9
Haitian	800	15,000	4.3	5,000	200,000	55.5
Nicaraguan	1,600	60,800	15.8	15,000	612,000	142.8
Guatemalan	450	10,000	3.2	5,000	120,000	30.9
El Salvadorian	560	10,000	3.5	4,000	160,000	42.1
Honduran	0	10,000	2.6	0	80,000	23.9
Overall	8,000	100,000	27.8	90,000	900,000	245.8

projection by national experts was slightly lower then the overall total projection of local experts for both 1989 and 1990–2000. However, the national total only included immigration from the target countries, while the local experts were asked to project overall immigration. If the estimates provided by national experts for other, nontarget countries are included, the 1989 national projection was almost precisely the same as the local projection, and the 1990–2000 national estimate was slightly higher then the local estimate. Overall, the consensus on total immigration levels is remarkable.

The national experts' forecasts suggested a slightly different mix of nationalities than was indicated by the local experts. The national experts, like the local experts, anticipated the largest share of immigrants will come from Nicaragua and that the second largest proportion will be Cuban. However, the national experts anticipated a larger segment coming from the other Central American countries than did local experts.

The national experts' "most likely" forecast was closer to the low forecast than to the high forecast for every nationality (Table 4.2). This suggests that experts see a relatively firm base level of immigration and a chance of large immigrant flows from the target countries occurring periodically throughout the decade.

The standard deviation of the forecasts is an indicator of the degree of disagreement among the experts concerning predicted levels. The larger the standard deviation, the greater the variation in the expert forecasts and the lower the level of agreement among experts. As one would expect, both the national experts and the local experts had much stronger levels of agreement when estimating short-term, 1989 immigration than when estimating

Table 4.2
Immigration Projections: National Experts (Median Estimates [Standard Deviation])

| Nationality | 1989 | | | 1990–2000 | | |
	Low	Most Likely	High	Low	Most Likely	High
Cuban	2,750 (3.1)	4,500 (3.1)	12,000 (6.5)	30,000 (27.5)	45,000 (26.3)	100,000 (66.1)
Haitian	2,250 (1.1)	3,500 (1.7)	7,500 (7.3)	15,000 (9.1)	32,500 (13.1)	75,000 (217.9)
Nicaraguan	12,500 (7.1)	22,500 (10.8)	40,000 (45.6)	90,000 (66.3)	125,000 (119.0)	180,000 (415.6)
Guatemalan	1,500 (1.2)	2,500 (1.5)	4,500 (3.9)	20,000 (15.4)	30,000 (18.9)	55,000 (39.0)
El Salvadorian	3,500 (1.4)	4,500 (1.7)	6,500 (3.3)	40,000 (17.3)	50,000 (24.5)	80,000 (68.5)
Honduran	1,500 (1.3)	2,500 (1.6)	4,500 (4.0)	15,000 (12.5)	25,000 (16.2)	45,000 (39.6)
Total	26,200 (9.2)	42,000 (12.2)	78,000 (63.6)	239,500 (98.0)	333,000 (129.6)	505,000 (823.0)
Other						
Colombia	3,000	4,000	5,000	40,000	70,000	90,000
Mexico	2,500	3,000	4,000	30,000	50,000	75,000
Russia	500	1,500	2,500	5,000	10,000	15,000

immigration levels for 1990–2000 (Table 4.3). Further, when these forecasts are compared to actual 1989 and 1990 documented immigration, they are very close to actual levels. The national experts also give more consistent projections when forecasting minimum or most likely levels of immigration than they do when attempting to forecast maximum immigration levels. High-end forecasts are more idiosyncratic. No doubt this reflects the fact that events precipitating large-scale immigration are more uncertain than the trends governing base-level immigration.

Further, the extent of agreement among forecasts by national experts varies substantially across nationalities. The highest level of disagreement concerned Nicaraguan, Cuban (for the low and most likely forecasts), and Haitian (for the high forecasts) immigration levels, both in the short and long term. There was a relatively high level of agreement concerning immigration levels from other Central American countries, although the consensus concerning the level of immigration from El Salvador eroded substantially for

Table 4.3
Comparison of National and Local Experts: Immigration Projections (Median
Number of Immigrants)

Nationality	1989			1990–2000	
	Local	National	Actual	Local	National
Cuban	8,750	4,500	5,733	70,000	45,000
Haitian	6,000	3,500	1,861	50,000	32,500
Nicaraguan	12,250	22,500	2,608	107,500	125,000
Guatemalan	2,500	2,500	443	20,000	30,000
El Salvadorian	2,500	2,500	558	30,000	50,000
Honduran	2,000	2,500	1,054	15,000	25,000
Other	1,260	3,000	12,312	107,500	
Overall	35,260	42,000	24,569	400,000	333,000

long-term forecasts. El Salvador was viewed by some of the experts as a potential source of large-scale immigration over the next decade.

The local experts had the highest level of disagreement over the number of Cuban and Nicaraguan immigrants in the long and short term. The level of disagreement concerning Haitian and Salvadorian immigration was fairly low in the short term, but increased substantially for the long-term forecast. From the results of the Delphi survey, experts forecasted that roughly 450,000 immigrants will enter Dade County and between 50,000 and 235,000 the City of Miami, over the next decade.

CHARACTERISTICS OF FUTURE IMMIGRANTS

In addition to the level of future immigration, experts were asked to predict specific characteristics of immigrants from Cuba, Haiti, Guatemala, El Salvador, Honduras, and other nonspecified target nations. Both expert groups were further asked to forecast specific immigrant characteristics that are likely to impact immigrant demands on local government services. Although more difficult to anticipate, both expert groups were much more willing to forecast future demands than they were to forecast future immigration levels.

Nationality

Experts were asked where most immigrants to the United States will come from during the 1990s. If the frequency of occurrence on the experts' lists is used as an indication of the certainty of substantial immigration, most future immigrants will be Mexican, Asian, Russian, Central American, or Caribbean.

Immigration in South Florida is anticipated by experts to be very different from U.S. immigration generally. The top sending countries for the United States do not accurately reflect the immigrant mix in the City of Miami. Experts forecast that the bulk of immigrants coming to Miami in the next decade will be from the Caribbean basin and Latin America. Immigrants from Asia, although expected to be a major component of immigration in the United States generally, are not expected by the experts to be an important source of immigration in Miami.

Differences between the local and national expert predictions provide interesting perspectives (see Table 4.4). For example, some local experts, but none of the national experts, mentioned Canada as a source of immigration. Similarly, a number of local experts mentioned non-Cuban Caribbean nations (specifically Jamaica and the Dominican Republic) and South American nations (such as Colombia, Peru, and Brazil) as significant sources of immigration. These nations were mentioned much less frequently by national experts.

Table 4.4
Primary Sources of Future Immigration: Number of Local and National Experts Responding to Individual Sources (Other than Cuba, Haiti, Nicaragua, Honduras, Guatemala, and El Salvador)

Country	Local	National	Total
Mexico	6	3	9
Colombia	6	2	8
Jamaica	4	2	6
Dominican Republic	4	1	5
Canada	4	0	4
Peru	3	0	3
Central America	2	5	7
Latin America	2	2	4
Europe	2	1	3
Brazil	2	0	2
Russia	2	0	2
Caribbean	1	4	5
Asia	1	0	1
Barbados	1	0	1
Panama	1	0	1
Venezuela	1	0	1
Paraguay	1	0	1
Argentina	1	0	1
Palestine	1	0	1
Hong Kong	1	0	1
China	1	0	1
Vietnam	1	0	1
Korea	0	1	1
Totals	48	21	69

National experts tended to be more vague than local experts, often providing regional or national areas, such as the Caribbean, South America, or Central America. This may reflect the difficulty that national experts have predicting immigrant mix at the local level.

Motivation for Immigrating

To provide follow-up regarding the nationality of future immigrants to the United States, both expert groups were asked why they expected immigrants to come from the countries they had listed. Political instability, economics, and U.S. government policies (both refugee and family reunification policies) were the most frequently cited reasons for emigrating (Table 4.5). Based on experts' judgment, a relatively larger number of future immigrants can be expected to be political or economic refugees. Unfortunately, virtually none of the factors listed by the experts as contributing to future immigration flow fall under the control of local government authorities.

Table 4.5
Causes of Immigration: National Experts

Cause	Frequency	(Percentage)
War and Political Oppression	14	(23.3)
Economic Problems in Native Country	12	(20.0)
Family Reunification Policies	8	(13.3)
U.S. Refugee Policies	6	(10.0)
Friends and Family in U.S.	5	(8.3)
Overpopulation in Native Country	4	(6.7)
Traditional Pattern in Native Country	4	(6.7)
U.S. Economic Opportunities	3	(5.0)
Geographic Proximity	1	(1.7)
U.S. Research Facilities	1	(1.7)
Availability of Transportation	1	(1.7)
Private-Sector Refugee Resettlement	1	(1.7)
Total	60	

Motivation for Choice of Residence Location

According to the experts, the primary factor affecting the immigrant's initial choice of residence in the United States is the existing distribution of countrymen. About two-thirds of the experts indicated that immigrants tend to move to areas where they will find others of their nationality. As previous chapters indicate, established colonies of immigrants tend to attract more immigrants to the area. Other factors noted by the experts include the following: friends and family in the area, past immigration patterns, economic opportunities, climate, geographical proximity, cost of living in the area, favorable public assistance, and U.S. resettlement policies (Table 4.6).

The list of factors emphasizes the self-reinforcing nature of immigration trends, and lends support for statistical modeling as an aid in forecasting immigration levels. Initial immigration into an area by a particular nationality draws fellow countrymen. Three of the top four factors used by the experts to predict residence patterns (i.e., attraction of fellow countrymen, clusters of kin, and past patterns) imply that past is prologue to future trends in immigration.

Table 4.6
Factors Influencing Immigrants' Choices of Residence Locations in the United States: National Experts

Cause	Frequency	(Percentage)
Existing Concentration of Countrymen	13	(31.0)
Friends and Family in Area	7	(11.9)
Past Immigration Patterns	7	(11.9)
Economic Opportunities	7	(11.9)
Climate	3	(7.1)
Geographical Proximity	2	(4.8)
Cost of Living in Area	1	(2.4)
Favorable Public Assistance	1	(2.4)
U.S. Resettlement Policies	1	(2.4)
Total	42	

Only two experts listed geographic proximity as a primary factor an immigrant uses in selecting a particular area to reside once in the United States. Other experts indicated that air transportation has minimized the importance of proximity as a residency determinant. Respondents also mentioned that government policies regarding relocation play a role in the immigrants' methods of entry and their short- and long-term locational desires. In addition, one expert suggested that national resettlement policies will have an impact on the distribution of immigrants, while other experts suggested that differences in public assistance policies could help explain the choice of residence by future immigrants.

In sharp contrast to the importance that federal policies were given by national experts in explaining the ultimate number of immigrants admitted to the United States, some local experts suggested that national immigration policies do not necessarily impact flows. This highlights a potential enclave phenomenon. It is a given that national policies have a major impact on the number of legal immigrants admitted into the United States annually, but these policies have virtually no impact on the distribution of immigrants within the United States. This enclave phenomenon is best witnessed by the relocation strategies employed by the federal government regarding the Mariel–Cuban entrants of 1980. The federal government established a resettlement program in which refugees were assigned to live in various states throughout the United States. However, within a short period, these refugees (or, if granted immigrant status, these residents) migrated back to the Miami community.

The list of factors underscores the lack of control by local governments over immigration. Not only do local governments have no control over the number of immigrants entering the United States, they also have limited control over the number of those immigrants settling in their jurisdiction. The only factor mentioned as affecting residential choice which local officials may impact is public assistance levels, and only one expert felt that this would impact the pattern of immigration and the number of immigrants residing in a particular area. Therefore, the consensus among the experts is that the most important factors determining immigration levels and choice of residence are outside the control of local authorities.

Documentation

According to both expert groups, the vast majority of immigrants from Cuba will be documented, and most immigrants coming from Haiti, Nicaragua, Guatemala, El Salvador, and Honduras will be undocumented (see Table 4.7). Roughly 20 percent of the experts felt that a majority of immigrants from these countries will be undocumented. A smaller percentage of the experts believed that the proportion of immigrants without documentation would fall below 25 percent over the next decade. Further, experts added a number of countries

Table 4.7
Proportion of Undocumented Immigrants (by Percentage): Local and National Experts Compared

Nationality	0-25%		26-50%		51-75%		76-100%	
	Nat.	Loc.	Nat.	Loc.	Nat.	Loc.	Nat.	Loc.
Cuban	5	22	1	4	--	--	--	--
Haitian	--	2	--	12	4	10	2	3
Nicaraguan	--	2	1	9	2	12	3	3
Guatemalan	--	3	2	6	2	12	2	5
El Salvadorian	--	3	1	5	3	12	2	6
Honduran	--	4	2	7	2	10	2	5

to the list indicated on the questionnaire. With the exception of Peru, undocumented immigrants are expected to make up less than half the total immigrants from all of these countries (Mexico, Jamaica, Columbia, Canada, Dominican Republic, Russia, Europe, Caribbean, and an unspecified other).

The national experts generally agreed with the local experts concerning a low proportion of undocumented aliens among Cuban immigrants, but foresee a higher proportion of undocumented immigrants among other immigrant pools. The difference is particularly noticeable for Haitian immigrants. All of the national experts expect at least 50 percent of Haitian immigrants to be undocumented, while less then half of the local experts anticipate that more than 50 percent of Haitian immigrants will be undocumented. It should be noted that only a few national experts were willing to attach specific numbers to these forecasts. Again, this indicates the reluctance of national experts to make local projections.

In addition, local experts disagreed among themselves about the proportion of undocumented immigrants (see Table 4.8). The local government administrators included in the Delphi survey generally anticipated a lower proportion of undocumented immigrants than did nongovernment service providers. The most extreme examples are forecasts of Honduran and Salvadorian undocumented immigration. None of the local government administrators expected more than one-quarter of immigrants from these countries to be undocumented, while half of the nongovernment service providers expected three-quarters or more of immigrants from Honduras and El Salvador to be undocumented. The government and nongovernment forecasts differ less for the other countries, but, in all cases except Cuba, the nongovernment service providers forecast a larger proportion of undocumented immigrants.

Table 4.8
Proportion of Undocumented Immigrants (by Percentage): Government
and Nongovernment Local Experts Compared

Nationality	0-25%		26-50%		51-75%		76-100%	
	Gov.	Non.	Gov.	Non.	Gov.	Non.	Gov.	Non.
Cuban	7	8	2	--	--	--	--	--
Haitian	--	1	4	5	5	2	--	1
Nicaraguan	1	--	4	3	4	4	--	1
Guatemalan	3	--	2	2	4	3	--	3
El Salvadorian	3	--	2	2	4	2	--	4
Honduran	4	--	2	2	3	2	--	4

This may reflect differences in the past experience of the nongovernment and government administrators. Undocumented immigrants are less likely to seek help from government because of concerns about eligibility and fears of apprehension. Therefore, alternative service providers would tend to see a higher number of undocumented immigrants, which, perhaps, more accurately reflects the actual population distribution.

Language

Virtually all of the experts indicated that less than 25 percent of the immigrants from the six countries targeted in the Delphi survey would be able to speak English upon arrival (Table 4.9). Most of the national and local experts agreed that English skills would be rare in these immigrant groups, and local governments should plan for such language difficulties. Both expert groups did predict better English skills among immigrants arriving from selected countries, however.

One expert noted a number of immigrants coming from Canada, and predicted that between 50 and 75 percent of these immigrants would be able to communicate in English. Other immigrant nationalities cited by experts as having between 50 and 75 percent English-speaking skills included Jamaica, Peru, and various European countries. Immigrants from other countries mentioned by the experts (Columbia, the Dominican Republic, Russia, and Mexico) were expected to include between 0 and 25 percent English speakers, though one expert predicted that the Mexican immigrants would include between 50 and 75 percent with English-language skills.

Table 4.9
Proportion of English-Speaking Immigrants (by Percentage): Local and National Experts Combined

Nationality	0-25%	26-50%	51-75%	76-100%
Cuban	28	3	1	1
Haitian	29	2	1	1
Nicaraguan	29	2	1	1
Guatemalan	29	2	2	--
El Salvadorian	30	1	2	--
Honduran	29	1	2	1
Others Added by Respondents				
Mexican	2		1	
Colombian	1			
Canadian			1	
Jamaican			1	
Dominican	1			
European			1	
Peruvian		1		
Russian	1			

Support Networks

Experts were asked what proportion of immigrants settling in the City of Miami would have established relatives, friends, or some other support network upon arrival (see Table 4.10). Most experts agreed that support networks would vary across nationalities. All of the experts indicated Cubans would have support networks upon arrival, and 85 percent of the experts felt that three-quarters or more of the Cubans would be enculturated into these networks. There was no difference between local and national experts regarding support networks for the Cuban immigrants.

The local experts were uncertain about the proportion of Haitian immigrants who will be greeted by a support network. While most of the experts expected at least half of the Haitian immigrants coming to the area will have friends, relatives, or other organizations available, nearly 10 percent thought less than one-quarter of the Haitians would have a network to greet them. Nearly 40 percent of the experts projected that less than half of the Haitians immigrants would have preexisting support networks when they arrive.

Table 4.10
Proportion of New Immigrants with Preexisting Support Networks (by Percentage): Local and National Experts Combined

Nationality	0-25%	26-50%	51-75%	76-100%
Cuban	--	--	5	28
Haitian	3	9	15	6
Nicaraguan	5	12	9	7
Guatemalan	15	14	2	2
El Salvadorian	15	13	2	3
Honduran	16	12	3	2
Others Added by Respondents				
Mexican		2	1	1
Colombian		1	1	
Canadian	1			
Dominican			1	
European	1			
Peruvian			1	
Russian	1			

When local government and nongovernment experts were compared, more than three-quarters of the local nongovernment service providers believed that at least 50 percent of the Haitians would be greeted by support networks, while only one-third of the local government administrators in the sample foresaw this many Haitians having preexisting support.

Regarding immigrants from Nicaragua, there is very little consensus among the experts about the proportion of Nicaraguans that will have a support network to tap upon arrival. The biggest grouping of respondents, about one-third of the entire sample, expect that between 26 and 50 percent of the Nicaraguan immigrants will have a support network. The national experts differ from the local experts in their expectations for Nicaraguan immigrant support networks. Over three-quarters of the national experts expect that at least 50 percent of the Nicaraguans will arrive with preexisting support networks, while less than half the local experts share this expectation.

In sum, experts expect that most, or virtually all, Cuban immigrants will have support networks when they arrive. They also predict (albeit with less consensus) that the majority of Haitians will have support networks, and that the bulk of the Guatemalan, Honduran, and Salvadorian immigrants will not have preexisting support networks. There is no consensus among the experts concerning the proportion of Nicaraguan immigrants having preexisting support networks.

Employment Skills

From the target countries identified through the first survey wave, the experts were asked to predict the proportion of future immigrants having white-collar skills, blue-collar skills, and no relevant job skills. According to the experts, none of the target immigrant groups can be expected to include a high proportion of immigrants with white-collar skills (Table 4.11). Cuban immigrants are, according to the experts, more likely to have white-collar skills, followed by Nicaraguans, and then other Central American immigrants (El Salvador, Guatemala, and Honduras). Haitian immigrants are expected to include the lowest proportion of immigrants with white-collar skills.

On average, experts expect a higher proportion of immigrants will have blue-collar skills. But there is little agreement among experts regarding the amount of immigrants with various skills. A sizable number of experts see a relatively small proportion (less than 25%) of immigrants having blue-collar skills, but, at the same time, some experts see nearly all the immi-

Table 4.11
Proportion of Immigrants with White-Collar Skills (by Percentage): Local and National Experts Combined

Nationality	0-25%	26-50%	51-75%	76-100%
Cuban	14	12	5	1
Haitian	31	1	--	--
Nicaraguan	19	10	3	--
Guatemalan	25	6	1	--
El Salvadorian	24	7	1	--
Honduran	26	4	1	--
Others Added by Respondents				
Mexican	3	1		
Colombian		1		1
Jamaican				
Dominican	1			
Peruvian			1	
Russian			1	

grants (more than 75%) as having these job skills. The median prediction forecast for each of the target nationalities is that 26 to 50 percent of the immigrants will have blue-collar job skills.

National experts, when compared to local experts, tended to anticipate a lower proportion of immigrants with blue-collar skills. The median value for local experts was the same as that for the entire pool of experts, predicting that between 26 and 50 percent of the immigrants (for all nationalities) would have blue-collar skills. The median forecast of the national experts was the same as that for local experts for Cubans, Haitians, Nicaraguans, and Salvadorans, but the national experts predicted that less then 26 percent of the Hondurans and Guatemalans will have blue-collar skills. Some local experts predicted over 75 percent of the immigrants from each target country would have blue-collar skills, a prediction that none of the national experts shared.

Most of the experts felt that the bulk of immigrants would arrive with some job skill applicable to the United States (Table 4.12). At least half of the experts predicted that three-quarters or more of the immigrants from Cuba, Nicaragua, Guatemala, Honduras, and El Salvador would have applicable job skills, and some experts predicted that three-quarters of the Haitian immigrants would arrive with an applicable job skill. On the other hand, 39 percent of the experts forecast that a majority of Haitian immigrants will

Table 4.12
Proportion of Immigrants with No Job Skills (by Percentage): Local and National Experts Combined

Nationality	0–25%	26–50%	51–75%	76–100%
Cuban	22	6	2	--
Haitian	12	7	7	5
Nicaraguan	16	8	3	3
Guatemalan	15	8	4	3
El Salvadorian	16	8	4	2
Honduran	15	9	4	2
Others Added by Respondents				
Mexican	3	1		
Colombian	2			
Dominican				1
Peruvian			1	
Russian	1			

have no relevant job skills, and about one out of five experts expected a majority of immigrants from Nicaragua, Guatemala, Salvador, and Honduras will have no applicable job skills.

National experts felt a somewhat higher proportion of immigrants would come without job skills than did the local experts. The local experts' median projected proportion of immigrants with no job skills was 26 to 50 percent for Haiti, and 0 to 25 percent for the other target nations. The national experts' median forecast was the same as that for local experts for Cuban and Haitian immigrants, but dropped for Nicaraguan and Salvadorian immigrants, and further fell for Hondurans and Guatemalans (i.e., the median prediction for the national experts suggests that between 26 and 50 percent of immigrants from Honduras and Guatemala will have no relevant job skills).

The local government administrators in the sample tended to forecast that a higher proportion of immigrants from the target countries would arrive without job skills than did the local nongovernment service providers. The median predictions of the two groups differed only for Haiti. The nongovernment service providers forecasted that 0 to 25 percent of the future Haitian immigrants will have no job skills, while the government administrators predict, on average, that 26 to 50 percent of the Haitians will have no relevant job skills (Table 4.13). But while none of the service-provider experts expected that more than 25 percent of the immigrants from any target country (except Haiti) would be without relevant job skills, nearly half of the government administrators in the sample felt that more than 25 percent of the immigrants from Nicaragua, Honduras, El Salvador, and Guatemala would have no relevant job skills.

Table 4.13
Proportion of Immigrants with No Job Skills (by Percentage): Government and Nongovernment Local Experts Compared

Nationality	0–25% Gov.	0–25% Non.	26–50% Gov.	26–50% Non.	51–75% Gov.	51–75% Non.	76–100% Gov.	76–100% Non.
Cuban	7	6	2	1	--	--	--	--
Haitian	4	6	1	1	2	--	2	1
Nicaraguan	5	7	3	--	--	--	1	--
Guatemalan	5	7	2	--	1	--	1	--
El Salvadorian	5	7	2	--	1	--	1	--
Honduran	5	7	2	--	1	--	1	--

DELPHI RESULTS: IMMIGRANT IMPACTS ON LOCAL GOVERNMENT

The results of the first expert survey wave indicated that experts felt immigration has had both positive and negative impacts on South Florida governments. When experts were asked about the impact of immigration on the local community, nearly half of the respondents commented on the positive effect on the economy (via inexpensive labor and increased international commerce). In addition, local experts indicated that the infusion of new ideas and energy from a group of people with high aspirations lends to the social and economic health of a community.

On the other hand, experts suggested that immigration had resulted in some communities bearing an unfair burden in addressing the needs of the immigrants, without adequate recompense. Experts suggested that, as a result of immigration, many communities had been divided into sometimes hostile subpopulations, increasing social tension in the community and creating problems in communication and government service provision. They saw local governments faced with increased demand for services and increased problems from drugs, crime, deteriorating housing, and a poorer local population. Despite the citing of these problems, the national experts were less pessimistic about immigration's impact. They tended to see the overall economic benefit to the community as far outweighing the negative impacts of short-term programmatic changes.

Respondents were asked to indicate the impact of immigration on the provision of specific government services, including police, emergency medical, water/sewage, waste disposal, fire, and total general government revenues and expenditures. Overall, experts agreed that local government services are strained as a result of unrestricted and uncontrolled immigrant waves. They disagreed as to whether incremental change impacts service requirements, since some felt that local governments can absorb a steady but small flow of individuals through the normal budgetary process. These experts felt that the effect of immigration is spread over time.

When immigration into a community occurs at a rapid rate, or a large number of immigrants enter within a short period, experts state that local governments are impacted quickly. In these situations, the impact becomes more apparent to the community at large, and service requirements are stepped up for the short term as a result of the perceived negative impact that immigrants have. In all, experts were in full agreement that immigrants are not drains on the local economy, as portrayed in the media and supported by local community beliefs. Experts were in full agreement that these suspicions are based on opinion rather than substantive analysis.

Many experts commented on the difficulties of multicultural administration. Several, primarily nongovernment respondents suggested that government has been slow to react to immigrant needs. Some saw immigrants as failing to understand the political and administrative system. One respondent noted that the experience of Haitians with government in Haiti substantially reduced their expectations for governmental assistance. Others argued that immigrant groups have a difficult time mobilizing political pressure.

A few respondents felt government had gone too far in accommodating immigrants. They were concerned that government was bending to the wishes of the immigrants, rather then insisting on the immigrants' accommodating themselves to the existing political-social-administrative structures and norms. One respondent noted a loss of cooperative abilities in government bodies. As the community becomes increasingly split, elected officials focus on small constituencies rather than the common good.

During the second round of the Delphi survey, the experts were asked to rate the impact of incoming immigrants (by nationality) on specific municipal services. A scale was devised based on a ranking of 1 (weak impact) to 7 (strong impact). Experts suggested that the strongest impact will be felt on general government revenues and expenditures, with little effect on other government funds (Table 4.14). The emphasis placed on general funds suggests that the respondents view immigration's impact as being on government overall, rather than as affecting individual services.

Nevertheless, there was some variance across specific service areas in forecasted immigrant impact. Impact is thought to be greatest for police services, followed by emergency medical services, water, sewer, and waste services. The respondents reported the lowest level of impact on fire services.

Table 4.14
Immigrant Impact on Municipal Services: National and Local Experts Combined

Immigrant Group	Police	Fire	EMS	Solid Waste	Water Sewer	Gov't Revenue	General Gov't
Cuba	5	3	4	4	4.0	5.0	6
Haiti	4	3	4	3	3.0	4.5	4
Nicaragua	4	3	4	3	3.0	5.0	6
Guatemala	4	3	3	3	3.5	4.0	4
El Salvador	4	2	3	3	2.5	5.0	4
Honduras	4	2	3	3	3.0	5.0	4
Sum	25	16	21	19	19.0	28.5	28

Note: Table entries reflect median score given by respondents on a seven-point impact scale, where 1 equals very little impact and 7 equals substantial impact.

Police

More than half of the experts argued that the impact on police services is largely a result of fear that immigrants will be criminals. As a result, local administrators act based on the assumption that immigrants lead to increased crime, which leads to increased workloads and therefore police personnel and jail-space requirements must be increased. Further, several respondents noted that the increased complexity of police work in dealing with cultural diversity and multiple languages impacts costs.

Many experts noted that part or all of the burden faced by the police department (as well as other services) was simply a consequence of increased population, rather then directly related to immigration. Several noted that, while there was a special burden placed on police services in Miami by immigration, it was a consequence of the Mariel immigrants and the high proportion of criminals in the Mariel population rather than immigration in general. Some of these respondents expressed concern that the public's and government's impressions of immigration effects would be unduly influenced by the Mariel experience. Normal immigration should not, in the view of a number of respondents, place an undue burden on police expenditures. One respondent commented on the positive effects of immigration on police services. They saw an increased flexibility, intelligence, and sophistication grow out of the police department's experience with immigration.

Criminal Activity

The experts expect a relatively low level of crime among future immigrants. Virtually all of the experts predicted that less than one-quarter of the future immigrants to the Miami area will engage in criminal activity (see Table 4.15). Depending on the immigrant nationality, 81 (Cuba) to 97 (Haiti) percent of the experts selected the 0 to 25 percent category as their forecast of the proportion of immigrants who will be engaged in criminal activity.

Several respondents noted that the proportion range was too large for this low-end category, and expressed concern that their forecast would be interpreted as suggesting that 25 percent of various immigrant populations might engage in criminal activities. The general tenor of the responses was that relatively few of the immigrants would engage in criminal activity. There were no real differences in forecasts provided by national and local experts and the forecasts of local government administrators and nongovernment service providers were similar.

Emergency Medical

Many respondents felt that emergency services had been affected by immigration to a greater extent than other local services. They suggested that

Table 4.15
**Proportion of Immigrants Engaging in Criminal Activity (by Percentage):
Local and National Experts Combined**

Nationality	0-25%	26-50%	51-75%	76-100%
Cuban	26	4	1	1
Haitian	30	1	1	--
Nicaraguan	27	5	--	--
Guatemalan	29	3	--	--
El Salvadorian	29	3	--	--
Honduran	29	3	--	--
Others Added by Respondents				
Mexican	4			
Colombian	2			
Jamaican		1		
Dominican	1			
Peruvian	1			
Russian	1			
Canadian	1			
European Community	1			

the poverty of immigrants, combined with their lack of familiarity with local doctors, low insurance coverage rate, and lack of personal transportation, leads to a much greater dependence on emergency medical services (EMS) by immigrants than by average citizens. Many experts suggested that emergency services are frequently called on by immigrants to deliver babies and handle other problems that are not generally requested by natives.

Several respondents noted an indirect impact on emergency medical services through immigration's (i.e., Mariel's) effect on crime. They saw an increase in emergency trauma cases. One respondent noted that "paramedics who have expertise with dealing with the heart attack victim have had to learn to deal routinely with the stabbing and gunshot victim."

As is the case with other services involving extensive interaction with citizens, several respondents note the impact of multiple languages. Difficulties in communication can make it more difficult to assist victims and sometimes frustrate EMS personnel.

Waste Disposal

Most respondents saw the impact of immigration on waste disposal as largely a function of population increase, but some noted special effects.

Experts noted cultural and national differences in waste-disposal practices, which place particular strain on local government. They cited differences in perceptions of sanitary disposal of trash and a lack of experience and education concerning U.S. systems for waste disposal leading to problems with litter and unsanitary waste disposal. One respondent, commenting on the impact of cultural norms on waste disposal, cited animal sacrifices as one example of a practice, brought by immigration, creating potential health problems. Another respondent, a local municipal political official (and an immigrant), described waste disposal as "the single most critical problem created by massive immigration."

A high-level administrator in a solid-waste department noted the problems with enforcement of waste-disposal ordinances (because of cultural differences in disposal practices), and the difficulties of educating the largely non-English-speaking immigrant population. The problem is aggravated, according to the respondent, by antibilingual sentiments, which inhibit the development and distribution of foreign-language service brochures. The additional costs of providing these services was also noted.

Fire Protection

According to respondents, immigration's impact on fire services has been less substantial then many of the other local services. Although a number of respondents noted the effects of simple population increase, respondents did not see any special burden for this service. Several high-level administrators in local fire departments cited a substantially increased burden, but saw it as almost entirely a consequence of the increase in demand for affiliated emergency medical services.

Water and Sewage

The increased demand on scarce water resources from the population increase attributable to immigration was discussed by a number of respondents. Only one respondent noted any special demand placed by immigrants, suggesting that water-usage habits varied across cultures and that some immigrant groups would have higher demand then others. The utilization of user fees for water consumption was viewed by most as moderating any adverse impact of immigration in this service area.

General Government Revenue

The respondents were split in their assessment of immigration's impact on overall government revenues. Most respondents indicated that local government revenues eventually rise because of the population increase from immigration and because of immigration's stimulation of the local economy.

A few felt there had been an actual decline in revenue as the economic base of the community was eroded by the influx of indigent immigrants, and a number of respondents felt that gains in revenues were clearly outdistanced by increased service demand. Many respondents noted that there is a lag between immigration and increases in general revenue. They felt that immigrants contribute little to government revenues initially, but over time they add significantly to the revenue base.

Some respondents argued that immigration has eroded the share of revenues allocated for assistance and services to the local minority groups, particularly the black population. Immigrants, according to this respondent, siphon off government revenues which would have otherwise gone to current resident populations. However, this sentiment was not consistently argued by other experts. In contrast, most experts stated that other lower-income groups are not adversely affected by immigration.

FUTURE IMMIGRATION POLICIES

In addition to estimating the number and characteristics of future immigrants, the national experts were specifically asked about the likelihood of future changes in U.S. policies affecting immigration. None of the experts felt that there would be an expansion of refugee eligibility criteria by 1990, but a small percentage of the experts felt that, within the next ten years, refugee status would be extended to immigrants currently not eligible. The experts identified immigrants from Nicaragua, Guatemala, El Salvador, Israel, Peru, and Honduras as those most likely to benefit from the refugee policy change, although only Nicaragua and El Salvador were named by more then one expert. Further, one expert stated that an extended voluntary departure policy would be established in the near or long term. The expert suggested that a national policy may be introduced shortly, and felt that it would probably encompass undocumented immigrants from Nicaragua, El Salvador, and Guatemala.

In response to an open-ended question asking about any additional policy changes effecting immigrants and immigration, one expert indicated that while "there is little sentiment in Washington for adopting policies that would encourage greater numbers of Central Americans to come to the U.S. . . . there might emerge some relief for those already illegally residing in the U.S., but it would likely be designed to discourage additional immigration."

Another expert predicted an increase in refugee flows in response to new legislation (such as safe haven) or an increase in documented immigrants through further liberalization of preference numbers and more liberal treatment of immediate relatives of current residents. Ultimately, according to experts, we can expect some kind of de jure or de facto "second amnesty" to legalize those now here who arrived after the passage of IRCA. Yet another expert foresaw policy reimbursing communities impacted by national immigration law, and seconded the likelihood of revision in preference and country limits for documented immigrants.

SUMMARY

The local and national Delphi surveys reflect a common view of future immigration flow and the likelihood of local control. Further, the case study shows that the local experts projected that 37,000 immigrants would arrive in 1989. This estimate was relatively close to the actual number of legal and undocumented immigrants in Miami during that year (27,000 legal and 6,000 undocumented). National experts gave more consistent forecasts when estimating minimum or most likely levels of immigration than they did when attempting to forecast maximum immigration levels. High-end forecasts are more idiosyncratic. No doubt this reflects the fact that events precipitating large-scale immigration are more uncertain then the trends governing base-level immigration.

Experts predicted that the vast majority of immigrants from "preferred" nations will be documented, and most of the immigrants coming from Haiti, Nicaragua, Guatemala, El Salvador, and Honduras will be undocumented. The nongovernment service providers, on average, expected a higher proportion of undocumented immigrants than did government administrators. This may reflect past experience with immigrant populations and therefore a more accurate assessment of the mix of immigrants residing in the area. Undocumented immigrants are less likely to seek help from government because of concerns about eligibility and fears of apprehension by authorities. The alternative service providers would tend to see a higher proportion of undocumented immigrants and, perhaps, a proportion more accurately reflecting the actual population distribution. Political instability, economics, and U.S. government policies (both refugee and family reunification policies) were the most frequently predicted reasons for immigration in the next decade.

The primary factor affecting immigrants' initial choice of residence in the United States will be the existing distribution of country persons. National policies are seen as having a major effect on immigration to the United States, but virtually no effect on the distribution of immigrants within the United States. None of the factors listed by the experts as contributing to future immigration falls under the control of local government authorities.

The two Delphi iterations found similar perceptions regarding the past impact of immigration on municipalities, both positive and negative. Both the national and local experts agreed on the positive effect of immigration on the economy (via inexpensive labor and increased international commerce) and on the addition of ideas and energy from a group of people with high aspirations. But respondents indicated that immigration had left local government faced with increased demand for services, increased problems from drugs and crime, and bearing an unfair burden in addressing the needs of the immigrants. However, the experts expected a relatively low level of crime among future immigrants. These sentiments were most noteworthy for the pool of local experts.

Most of the local government administrators and about 50 percent of the respondents overall predicted an increased financial burden on all local government services. The profusion of cultural differences accompanying immigration has also created problems in communication and government service provision that cut across service areas.

In sum, only 10 percent of the experts, none of them municipal administrators, predicted that future immigration would not be a serious problem for municipal service provision. As a group, the respondents suggested that the strongest impact will be felt on general government revenues. In order to mitigate future impact from immigration, most of the municipal administrators and nearly half of all respondents called for increased federal assistance. Further, about 35 percent of the respondents stressed the need for proper management of growth to ensure environmental resources and continued quality of life are maintained.

This chapter demonstrated the utility of a Delphi survey for obtaining national and local information regarding service-level impacts and immigration forecasts. The issue of forecasting immigration will be returned to in Chapter 6. Combined with the immigrant surveys technique covered in Chapter 3, a rich amount of data concerning the dynamics of immigration and informed impressions regarding immigration impacts on municipalities is obtained. The cost to municipalities for both efforts is seen to be mostly in man-hours. The survey skills needed will be found in most planning departments. What is left unaddressed to this point is the actual monetary impact of immigration on cities. Our case study experts felt that there are both financial costs and gains associated with immigration. As the revenue and expenditure impact is felt by many to be the central issue regarding immigration, and as it is an empirical question, Chapter 5 will demonstrate the empirical analysis of the monetary effect of immigration on municipal revenues and expenditures, guided by hypotheses developed from the literature review and Delphi survey findings.[7]

NOTES

1. Their contribution to this research effort will be demonstrated in Chapter 6, when the focus shifts to forecasting immigration levels and their potential future impact on municipalities.

2. Although the response rate from a statistical vantage was questionable, the literature demonstrates that a group of fifteen to twenty experts suffices for reaching asymptotic efficiency.

3. The national experts ranged in age from twenty to seventy-one years, with a majority having a graduate degree, although all had at least some college experience.

The majority were white (15), with one black, one Asian, and two who did not report ethnicity. Two were first-generation and six were second-generation immigrants. Most speak, read, and write Spanish or French as well as English. They included five academics, three working in research institutes, one politician, and six high-level government administrators, including representatives of the Department of State, the INS, and the Bureau of the Census.

The local experts ranged in age from twenty-eight to eighty years, with fifteen holding graduate degrees and all having at least some college experience. The respondents included three lawyers, six representatives of immigrant organizations or nonprofit service-delivery units, two political officials, one local representative of the INS, and thirteen high-level administrators in local government organizations, including four in local fire or fire rescue divisions, four in police departments, one in economic development, one in a public works department, and three in local general administration. The majority were white (22), with two black, and one unreported. Six respondents reported being first-generation immigrants and five indicated they were second-generation immigrants. Approximately thirteen speak, read, and write Spanish, while some speak, read, and write French; a few know Creole and Portuguese in addition to English. They had lived in South Florida anywhere from seven and a half to fifty years.

4. The definition of immigrant in this context included both documented and undocumented aliens.

5. Twenty of the local experts provided 1989 forecasts, and sixteen provided estimates for 1990–2000. The decline in response is indicative of the trepidation that experts felt in being asked to predict something as complex as future immigration.

6. The responses suggest that a better question might be, "What impact on crime rates would occur due to the immigration of various groups?" This would allow for the fact that some groups may contain a small proportion of high-rate offenders (as in the 1980 Mariel Boat Lift) and that immigrants are often victims of crime.

7. The statistical skills needed for the analysis in Chapter 5 can be found in many city budget and finance offices.

CHAPTER 5

Effects of Immigration on Municipal Revenue and Expenditures: Estimates and Implications

Documenting the impacts of immigration on local government revenue and expenditure capacity is problematic for many reasons. First, few municipal organizations have maintained long-term records concerning service utilization.[1] This stems from many factors, but for most municipal services, data on immigrant usage are very difficult and costly to collect. Even if some method of isolating the use of these services by immigrants could be developed (such as yearly sampling of park visitors or documenting criminal offenses by immigrant status), the data would indicate little about the indirect and secondary effects of immigration on service use and provision.

Difficulties relating revenue and expenditure data to immigrant impacts also abound. Many public services can absorb additional consumers with little or no effect on resources. The swimming pool at a local park, for example, is available for all, and an additional user may only marginally impact revenues and expenditures for that facility. However, unusually large immigration levels may eventually tax resources and facilities sufficiently enough to require additional operating and capital expenditures. The problem, for longitudinal purposes, is that the financial effect may be well after the original immigration influx. Therefore, sorting out short-term and long-term impacts is critical to understanding the total financial impact of immigration. Further complicating the determination of impacts, local government financial indicators are typically not archived long enough for longitudinal purposes.

Another compounding influence in attempting to establish impacts is that municipal resource levels are a function of many factors other than immigration. The range of factors affecting resources increases variability and makes it more difficult to discern immigration impacts. For example, municipalities typically have reserve resources for emergencies, either as departmental reserves or other unencumbered revenues (e.g., the "rainy-day account"). Immigration may have a financial impact, but one which cannot be seen because a local government is forced to utilize these reserve funds. The problems are further accentuated by the broad array of departmental categories used in municipal financial data. The categories allow for considerable shifting of programmatic efforts, with little apparent impact on total city-wide expenditures. Expenditures or revenues may actually move in and out of the budget through the creation of special taxing districts, transferring functions across the intergovernmental spectrum, or shifting objects of expenditures within programs, thus masking major substantive impacts.

Three additional factors may potentially limit the determination of financial impacts. The first and most central dimension is that municipalities are not allowed to deficit finance, and are constrained by state laws as to the type and amount of taxes to be collected in any given period. Therefore, additional service requirements may have less influence on the overall growth of expenditures than does the level of resources available to finance them. Immigration's effect may be masked, to some degree, by the pressure to suppress expenditures in any given period due to revenue constraints.

Second, immigration's effect on services may be qualitative rather than quantitative. Large levels of immigration may stretch the municipality thin, but impacts may appear through long-term quality erosion rather than incremental changes in revenues or expenditures. Further, employees can act as shock absorbers; able to increase their work effort when required and thus minimizing short-term measurable impacts. However, long-term effects become more severe if employees burn out or quit to take more stable and less demanding jobs. Last, many of the programs most directly affected by immigration, such as mandated social service programs, are solely financed and controlled by municipal governments.

These caveats suggest that it will be difficult to isolate immigration effects on revenues and expenditures. Conversely, if impacts are exposed, they should be interpreted at the lower boundary, since so many variables intrude in the direct evaluation of impacts.

Given the various challenges that have been identified regarding the ability to isolate immigrant impacts on local governments, a multiple research method is utilized to develop baseline revenue and expenditure data. Building on the findings of the literature review and the Delphi survey, this chapter suggests hypotheses to frame the quantitative assessment of financial impacts. Longitudinal archival data from the Census of Governments, INS, and local services are then used to construct and evaluate revenue and expenditure patterns.

DATA

Since direct measures of municipal public service use by immigrants are limited, the best available indicators for municipal expenditures and revenues are generated by the Federal Bureau of Census, which compiles various data bases from state and local reports. These data can be disaggregated for specific municipal revenue and expenditure categories. In addition to secondary sources of information, local governments often have a rich source of primary data to draw upon. Even though most municipalities have not directly measured immigration impacts, they have maintained historical information which proves valuable in documenting impacts. A constraint to this information is the limited time period over which the data have typically been collected on the local level.

For revenue and expenditure analysis, the data may include finance reports, budget documents, and appropriations legislation. Like most municipalities, the City of Miami has never formally attempted to measure the financial impact of immigration, nor has the city developed sufficient data, such as surveys, locational sampling, or service demands, to conduct a thorough empirical investigation. Few cities attempt to keep track of immigration levels, and the immigration numbers used in this phase of the analysis were developed via the estimation techniques discussed in Chapter 2.

ANALYTICAL METHODS

City of Miami immigration levels are related to revenues and expenditures using bivariate correlations and polynomial distributed-lag regression (Pindyck and Rubinfeld, 1981). Although on the surface the quantitative methods seem intractable, their application is relatively straightforward. The bivariate correlation technique associates overall immigration levels with changes in revenues and expenditures for the year of entry and each subsequent year through the eight-year study horizon, holding all other factors constant.[2] This method can be used to compare per capita and absolute figures, as well as to analyze impacts over time using inflation-adjusted dollars (constant dollars).

In the distributed-lag analysis, arrival levels are regressed on changes in absolute and per capita revenues and expenditures. Both the bivariate and distributed-lag analyses yield estimates of the initial impact of aggregate immigration during a given year t, and the impact of year t immigration on revenues and expenditures in subsequent years. Several alternative model specifications are used to derive impacts and produce estimates. In all, the third-degree polynomial was the most consistent model employed. In those situations where a different specification was utilized, indication is provided regarding the length of lag (i.e., the length of time necessary for impacts to emerge).

It is important to note, however, that the dynamics of revenues and expenditures are influenced by many factors, and immigration may or may not be one of the primary factors. The techniques employed simply do not provide for such conjecture. As demonstrated by the prior steps, however, it is assumed for this analysis that immigration is important.

Although the techniques discussed herein are not used to draw causal inferences about immigration's impact on a local government's financial position, the methods provide useful information about the possible association between the growth in population resulting from immigration and its relation to changes in revenues and expenditures. In addition, the statistical techniques can lend empirical support to the Delphi findings. More specifically, if a particular revenue source or expenditure demonstrates a relationship with changes in immigration, and the direction of the relationship is consistent with expert opinion, we become more confident in both the qualitative and quantitative evidence that a relationship exists. Further, reviewing previous research findings which support these results also provides support for claims that immigration has a relationship with certain municipal revenue and expenditure considerations.

The distributed-lag models can be used to calculate the overall effect of estimated immigration on revenue and expenditure impacts in a given year. The 1989 change in general expenditures associated with immigration, for example, can be calculated by summing 1989 effects of immigrants arriving during the preceding eight years.[3] The effects of immigration in prior years is calculated by multiplying the number of immigrants arriving in that year by the associated lag coefficient; for example, multiplying the estimated number of immigrants arriving in 1989 by the lag_0 coefficient, the number arriving in 1988 by the lag_1 coefficient, 1987 arrivals by the lag_2 coefficient, and so on through 1981 arrivals which are multiplied by the lag_8 coefficient (see Table 5.1 for coefficients). Thus, Table 5.2 shows the calculation for 1979 for GENEXP (General Expenditures) using the 1971–1979 immigration figures from Chapter 2.

USING HYPOTHESES FOR EMPIRICAL ANALYSIS

Hypotheses are one tool for structuring more detailed analyses. The amount of data in various forms can be overwhelming, and the development of a priori hypotheses provides a framework for proceeding from data collection to data analysis and interpretation. In addition, the use of hypotheses can assist administrators in defining and refining their beliefs, and can pro-

Table 5.1
Change in Deflated Revenues and Expenditures for Miami: Correlated (Kendall Tau) with Lagged Total Immigration

	\multicolumn{9}{c}{Lagged Total Immigration}								
	Lag_0	Lag_1	Lag_2	Lag_3	Lag_4	Lag_5	Lag_6	Lag_7	Lag_8
REVENUES									
GENREV	-.11	-.01	-.12	.12	.30[b]	.21	.03	.17	-.09
PROPTAX	-.14	-.14	-.30[b]	-.07	.08	.14	.10	.09	-.06
SALESTX	-.12	.02	.03	.02	-.04	-.01	-.05	.16	.04
REVUTIL	.28	.37[b]	.18	.01	-.08	.03	.49[b]	.56[b]	.33
CHRGREV	-.26[b]	-.17	-.23[a]	-.16	-.15	-.06	-.01	-.17	-.17
IGTOT	-.13	.03	-.05	.17	.16	-.11	.11	.09	-.06
IGSTAT	-.08	.04	-.05	.12	.33[b]	.08	.09	.16	-.00
IGFED	-.19	.18	.05	-.01	.09	-.16	.17	.27[a]	.00
EXPENDITURES									
GENEXP	.03	.17	-.01	-.01	.21	.05	.06	.26[a]	.03
PERSONNEL	.02	-.01	-.04	.21	.21	.05	-.07	.00	-.00
CAPITAL	.19	.21	-.08	-.05	.08	.08	.09	.21	.01
POLICE	-.14	.21	.14	.03	.12	.05	-.04	.04	-.05
FIRE	-.09	.00	.14	-.07	.09	.04	.00	.21	.15
GARBAGE	-.03	.08	-.04	.10	.10	-.02	.12	.18	-.03
PARKREC	.10	.18	-.10	-.18	-.03	-.04	.18	.21	-.03
STREETS	-.08	.05	-.03	-.01	.13	.21	.04	.26[a]	.16
SEWER	.13	-.01	-.07	.11	.25	-.10	-.05	.08	.19
GENGOVT	-.14	-.24[a]	.04	.05	-.00	.17	.01	-.10	.02
FINADM	-.23	-.35[b]	-.09	-.02	.05	.14	-.19	-.16	.02
GENCON	-.18	-.19	-.08	-.34[b]	-.25[a]	.06	.22	.02	-.06
PUBBLDG	-.09	.06	-.09	.07	.14	-.05	.23	.25[a]	.03

Note: Lags are based on one-year increments. That is, with lag_0, financial data are being correlated with immigration of the same year; with lag_2, financial data are being correlated with immigration two years earlier.
[a] $p < 0.10$
[b] $p < 0.05$

Table 5.2
Immigration Lagged for GENEXP

Year	Level	Coefficient	Impact
79	13022	.01	$ 130
78	9286	.15	1393
77	10321	-.03	-309
76	9041	-.03	-271
75	15325	.23	3525
74	20177	.08	1614
73	9621	.06	577
72	15738	.25	3935
71	25700	.07	1799
Total Impact			$ 12393

vide a mechanism for empirically examining the relative merits of claims, rather than simply relying on speculation or rhetoric. The hypotheses from the Miami case study follow the same pattern as the Delphi surveys and break the revenue and expenditure impacts into functional categories. Within each revenue and expenditure option, hypotheses are provided which set the stage for interpreting empirical results and evaluating the consistency of Delphi findings.[4] This chapter continues with the eight hypotheses and a brief look at the results.

REVENUES

According to recent analysis of local government revenue portfolios, *ad valorem* property taxes continue to be the primary source of local government own-source revenues (McCue, 1993). The second largest source, and still accounting for a significant portion of local government portfolios, are intergovernment revenues. The third, and growing in prominence, are user charges and charges for services. These three major sources are followed by fines, forfeitures, and miscellaneous revenues. Although the level of analysis evaluated below is broad, it provides benchmarks that allow further detailed analysis to unfold.

The categories analyzed in the case study include all of the major revenue sources used by most municipalities throughout the United States, except for the local income tax (see Table 5.3). Given that Florida has no income tax, this important revenue source is not analyzed. However, since the total revenues of the city are analyzed, this limitation may not artificially skew results.

Property Taxes

Due to the inherent slow nature of property tax appraisal systems, property tax revenues will be slower to react to immigration than other population-sensitive revenue sources. However, property tax revenues should, as experts indicated, increase along with property values as immigrants become settled and add to the demand for housing.

Hypothesis 1: Throughout the time horizon of the study, property tax revenues are positively impacted by immigration. The analysis links immigration to small losses in property tax revenues for the year of entry and the next four years (with the losses peaking at $73 per immigrant the year after entry), followed by three years of small gains in deflated property tax revenues (peaking with an increase of $29 per immigrant six years after entry). Overall, the model reflects a net loss of $214 per immigrant ($260 in 1989 dollars) in deflated property tax revenues during the first eight years after entry (Table 5.4).

Therefore, in contrast to the original hypothesis and Delphi findings, immigration has a net negative effect on property tax revenues for the Miami

Table 5.3
Change in City of Miami Revenues Attributable to Immigration (Millions of 1989 Dollars)

						Year					
Revenue	79	80	81	82	83	84	85	86	87	88	89
General	27.5	8.1	8.7	22.0	31.4	34.0	30.4	21.2	15.2	18.9	11.1
Property Tax	-3.8	-5.9	-6.7	-7.1	-5.5	-3.3	-2.0	-1.6	-2.6	-5.6	-4.3
Sales Tax	1.6	4.0	3.9	2.1	0.3	-0.0	0.8	2.4	3.3	2.4	1.7
Utility Tax	6.4	6.2	6.3	6.2	6.5	7.0	7.1	6.8	5.8	4.2	4.2
User Fees	-5.7	-6.0	-6.2	-6.5	-5.7	-4.9	-4.7	-4.7	-5.1	-6.1	-4.0
Intergovernmental Revenue											
Total	26.8	22.6	22.1	20.8	25.8	32.3	34.7	33.2	25.4	10.4	15.1
State	15.3	14.1	14.3	12.9	16.8	21.1	21.8	20.0	13.8	3.1	9.8
Federal	11.5	8.5	7.8	7.9	9.0	11.2	12.9	13.2	11.6	7.3	5.3

Table 5.4
Selected Revenue Sources Starting in Year of Arrival

Year	Property Tax	Sales Tax	Intergov't Revenue	Charges for Services	Utility Tax	Total General Revenue
0	$ -54.99	$ 44.32	$ -66.97	$ -20.60	$ 4.05	$ -274.30
1	-73.11	34.36	-36.98	-30.37	14.11	-177.37
2	-64.68	5.33	54.08	-32.26	27.20	56.42
3	-39.98	-18.60	170.35	-29.19	40.37	263.83
4	-9.34	-24.33	275.94	-24.13	50.63	352.82
5	16.95	-9.82	334.97	-20.01	55.04	302.55
6	28.59	15.93	311.58	-19.78	50.62	163.32
7	15.26	32.84	169.88	-26.37	34.40	56.64
8	-33.32	9.79	-126.00	-42.74	3.42	175.19
Total	$ -214.62	$ 89.82	$1086.85	$-245.45	$ 279.84	$ 919.10

host community. This finding potentially supports the view that, as immigrants become more economically sufficient, they move from their original host community to other more prosperous communities, typically in the suburbs. Unfortunately, due to data constraints, we were unable to pursue this alternative hypothesis.

Intergovernment Revenues

Since the early 1970s, a bulwark of intergovernment revenues has been tied to funding formulas. These formulas stress geographic dispersion, population, and, in some cases (notably block or categorical grants), measures of the community's well-being or poverty level. Legal immigration's direct effect on population growth is expected to impact formula-driven revenues. This occurs only after the entity providing assistance officially recognizes the additional immigrants. It is important to note that it is official estimates of population and poverty which are used for dispersing intergovernment revenues. This is particularly important for jurisdictions potentially experiencing large undocumented populations. If these individuals are not officially accounted for in determining intergovernment revenues, a jurisdiction suffers the financial burden of these individuals without compensation from higher levels of government.

Further complicating the immigration–intergovernment revenue relationships is the tendency for immigration to come in waves. Several radical, erratic shifts in the number of immigrants arriving in the United States have occurred throughout history. These peaks and valleys are difficult to take into account between decennial census enumerations, and are more difficult to account for in funding formulas.

Hypothesis 2: Immigrants' impact on intergovernment revenues occurs after a lengthy lag. Overall, intergovernment revenues from both federal and state sources show limited association with immigration in the correlational analysis. There appears to be a small decline during the year of arrival, followed by an increase during the third and fourth years after arrival.

The distributed-lag model predicting immigration's effect on total intergovernment revenues suggests somewhat stronger relationships. Both federal and state assistance (deflated) show a small decline the year of arrival (a drop of $29 per immigrant in state aid and $41 per immigrant in federal aid) and the next year (a $3 decline in state aid and $40 drop in federal aid). State aid begins to increase the second year after entry and peaks during the fifth year, when an estimated $215 per immigrant is added through state assistance. Federal aid begins to increase the third year after entry and the increases peak during the sixth year, when an estimated $131 per immigrant is added through federal assistance.

Over the eight-year period, the average immigrant is associated with an increase of about $700 ($855 in 1989 dollars) in state aid and about $420 ($507 in 1989 dollars) in federal aid. As originally argued, there is a considerable lag between entry and intergovernment revenue enhancement. In fact, the net impact of an immigrant on state assistance is negative for the first two years (including the year of entry) and the average immigrant is associated with a net decline in federal assistance for the first four years.

Sales Tax Revenues

Bivariate correlations suggest immigration is associated with a small decline in sales tax revenue during the year of arrival and small increases during the next six years. The distributed-lag model examining the immigration–sales tax revenue mix is more in line with initial expectations. This model indicates an initial increase in revenues classified as sales tax ($44 per immigrant the first year, $34 the second, and $5 the third) followed by three years of sales tax revenue reductions and then three more years of modest immigration-related increases (although no increases or decreases are statistically significant). The model suggests a modest net increase ($108 in 1989 dollars) in sales tax revenue over the eight years following the arrival of an immigrant.

User Fees and Charges for Services

Immigration (documented and undocumented) adds immediately to the population using these services. The effect on demand may be lagged to a small extent, as immigrants get to know municipal services and their ability to pay improves. Further, immigration may have a secondary effect on user fees through its impact on subsequent population flows. The primary positive effect may be offset if the immigrant flow results in a corresponding movement of existing residents out of the municipality, or if the immigrants leave the local jurisdiction once they are established (similar to the findings regarding property tax revenues). The positive effect may be reinforced if initial immigration leads to additional immigration in later years.

Hypothesis 3: User fees (utility charges in particular) will be affected quickly by immigration. Findings indicate that user fees have a mixed relationship with immigration. Correlation analysis suggests immigration in a given year is associated with a rather strong increase in utility revenues during the year of entry and for the next two years. Immigration in a given year is also associated with a strong increase in utility revenues six, seven, and eight years after immigrants arrive. Perhaps immigrants become settled and use more utilities during this later period, or perhaps, as immigrants become settled, their consumption habits change. Analysis was not conducted to support either scenario.

The "best-fit" third-order distributed-lag model indicates larger increases in utility revenue peaking the fifth year after entry (from a $5 increase the year of arrival to a peak increase of $55 the fifth). Overall, the model suggests the average immigrant adds nearly $300 ($339 in 1989 dollars) to deflated utility revenue over the eight-year period.

General Revenues

The literature examining the impact of immigration on the financial resources of local governments often analyzes specific revenue sources such as those identified previously. By including the total general-fund revenues, new insights into the impact can unfold. It is assumed from specific trends of individual revenue sources that the overall trend will be positive for the host community. That is, immigrants generate additional tax revenues for the general fund, holding all else constant.

Hypothesis 4: Immigration's effect on total general government revenues is positive, but this net benefit will occur several years after an immigrant arrives. The main effect of immigration on the City of Miami's overall general revenue is positive, but occurs several years after the immigrant's arrival. Bivariate analysis of the pattern of immigration and revenue fluctuations in the City of Miami associates immigration with small declines in general revenue (adjusted for inflation) the year the immigrant arrives and the next two years. This period is followed by relatively large increases in general revenue during the third, fourth, and fifth years.

Estimation of lagged effects of overall immigration on Miami's general revenue was also analyzed using an eight-year distributed-lag model.[5] Based on a fourth-degree Almon polynomial and the restriction that the effect of immigration in a given year on the previous year's revenue be fixed at zero, the model explained 21 percent of the variation in changes in deflated general revenue.[6] The estimated model for general revenue is very similar to the bivariate correlations.[7] The estimate for Miami linked immigration to revenue losses during the year of arrival (averaging $274 per immigrant) and the next year ($177 per immigrant), followed by yearly revenue increases during the rest of the study period (with revenue increasing, on average, $56 the second year after entry, $264 the third, $353 the fourth, $303 the fifth, $163 the sixth, $57 the seventh, and $175 the eighth year after entry). The loss of revenue in the first two years is more than made up over the next three and, when immigration's impact is viewed over the entire study period, it is associated with a net increase in general revenues (after inflation) of $920 ($1,118 in 1989 dollars) per immigrant.[8]

As demonstrated, the pattern of effects varies across components of general revenue, and therefore local governments that rely on a particular revenue source different than those analyzed here may experience very different impacts. That is, if the local government conducting an impact analysis were to rely almost exclusively on property taxes, the overall determination may be an actual decline in revenues for a longer period of time. Further, an immigrant's overall impact could well be marginal in such a municipality.

EXPENDITURES

For analytical purposes, expenditures will be examined based on two classification schemes. The first perspective examines immigration's impact on general government objects of expenditures. These categories include personnel expenses, operating expenses, and capital expenditures. The category of personnel comprises salaries for both full- and part-time employees and fringe benefits, including FICA, Social Security, health insurance, pension contributions, overtime if appropriate, and workers' compensation costs. Operating expenditures are all those costs associated with a department or program that are neither personnel or capital expenditures. Capital expenditures include items of a fixed nature that, for operating purposes, have not been included in a separate capital budget.

In addition to the categories discussed previously, this section analyzes immigration's impact on specific programs. All of the services analyzed are included in the general fund of the city. Moreover, two enterprise activities are studied to demonstrate potential impacts and exhibit the usefulness of the technique. The major purpose for including the enterprise activities is to demonstrate that the techniques are applicable across all government fund types.

Personnel Expenditures

As the level of immigration into a community increases, it is anticipated that the number of government employees providing services should increase as well. This relationship is relatively unambiguous. For example, when the population in a municipality increases as a result of immigration and demands for services increase (such as the number of police calls responded to in a given period), additional personnel must be hired. In some service areas, like parks and recreation, the additional demand may not be as apparent and the infusion of resources may not be as dramatic.

In addition to hiring more personnel, a local government may respond to increased service demands by increasing overtime expenditures. When an immigrant enters the community and the population increases, service demands increase for most areas, and, therefore, personnel expenditures increase. The impact may not be felt the first year of arrival; instead, the impact is spread over a period of time. That is, in any particular year the number of immigrants entering the municipality will not drastically impact the demands for services. However, additional service demands placed by new immigrants over time, coupled with demands of immigrants of previous years, leads local governments to respond by hiring additional personnel.

Hypothesis 5: The costs for personal services are not directly felt due to steady immigration, but during periods of large immigration, personnel expenditures are felt almost immediately. The correlational analysis, as posited, suggests that changes in personnel service costs are not highly associated with either documented immigration or estimated overall immigration throughout the study period. Further, the distributed-lag models for personnel services are in accord with prior expectations (Table 5.5). The category is estimated using third-degree polynomials, and immigration is only

Table 5.5
Expenditures by Category Starting in Year of Arrival

Year	Personal	Other	Capital	Total Expenditures
0	$ 54.38	$ -70.23	$ -26.32	$ -42.17
1	92.11	-92.28	-24.03	-24.20
2	114.88	-79.95	-0.91	35.02
3	124.38	-47.02	35.27	112.63
4	122.30	-7.32	76.76	191.74
5	110.32	25.41	115.76	251.49
6	90.14	37.33	144.53	272.00
7	63.45	14.66	155.28	233.39
8	31.94	-56.42	140.26	115.78
Total	$ 803.90	$ -275.82	$ 616.60	$1,144.68

able to explain about 8 percent of the variance in this type of expenditure, as shown by the low correlations.

The model predicting changes in personal services suggests immigration is associated, although not statistically significant, with increases in deflated personnel expenditures throughout the study period. Deflated personnel service expenditures increase by $54 per immigrant in the year of arrival, $92 the next year, $115 the second year after arrival, $124 the third, $122 the fourth, and $110 the fifth, with the yearly increases declining to $32 per immigrant eight years after arrival. Overall, immigration in a given year is estimated to increase deflated personnel services expenditures by $802 ($974 in 1989 dollars) per immigrant within nine years of entry.

Operating Expenditures

Operating expenditures include such items as supplies, travel, publications, uniforms, repair and maintenance of equipment, and all items and services that are directly linked to the operations of the organizational unit, but are not classified as personnel or capital expenditures. It is assumed that immigration forces local governments to employ expenditure-reducing or -dampening activities, and early in the process operating expenditures fall victim.

Given the limited time frame for this analysis, the reductions in operating expenditures will not be offset by later increases due to the fact that once these items are reduced, the tendency of local governments is to delay increases if there are no signs of increased revenues (i.e., the balanced budget constraint).

Hypothesis 6: Operating expenditures are negatively impacted by immigration throughout the time horizon of the case study. The results reported in

Table 5.5 demonstrate the variability of this expenditure category. When immigrants enter a community and administrators pursue avenues to reduce overall expenditures in order to shift resources to personal services, operating expenditures are reduced. In fact, the nature of the relationship exhibits that, for the first five years after entry, operating expenditures are reduced by $70.23, $92.28, $79.95, $47.02, and $7.32, respectively. However, when the demand for personnel begins to stabilize or decrease, local governments once again infuse additional resources for these expenditures to make up for poor past funding habits, or are forced to increase operating expenditures to ensure that programs are carried forward.

Capital Expenditures

When local governments are confronted with increased service demands and operate under resource constraints, they often turn to operating and capital items for reduction. For capital purposes, this can come in many forms, but predominantly the decision focuses on either the delay of the acquisition of capital, such as computers or office furniture, or the delay of capital maintenance, which may or may not be classified as an operating expenditure. Therefore, immigration may not have a strong negative impact for the first couple of years on capital expenditures, in that resources can be shifted from this category to fund personnel costs. Eventually, the delay reaches a point that many infrastructure items simply must be funded or fall apart. Therefore, a positive impact may come many years after the arrival of an immigrant.

Hypothesis 7: Capital expenditures will be immediately impacted by immigration, but eventually expenditures will rise as the municipal infrastructure and capital demands come under increasing population pressure. Empirical examination of the hypothesis predicting deflated capital expenditures suggests that immigration is associated with a decrease in capital expenditures for the year of entry (an estimated decrease of $26 per immigrant) and the first two years after entry (estimated decreases of $24 and $1, respectively). From the third year after entry through the eighth year, immigration is associated with increases in capital expenditures (the largest increase, $155, occurs seven years after entry). By the fourth year, deflated capital expenditures return to (and surpass) preimmigration levels. Overall, immigration in a given year is estimated to increase capital expenditures by a total of $617 ($750 in 1989 dollars) per immigrant within nine years of entry.

SERVICE LEVEL IMPACTS

As the three object-of-expenditure hypotheses (5, 6, and 7) indicate, immigration's impact on the type of expenditures is not overly conclusive. A potential reason for this finding is that local governments, acting under budget constraints (revenues must equal expenditures), do not shift resources between objects, like personnel and capital, but instead move resources across services. Rather than shift dollars from capital to personnel, local governments may identify certain program areas that are anticipated to be impacted quickly, like public safety, where additional resources must be infused. Among those services that may not feel impacts immediately, resources may increase over time to offset previous declines. Therefore, increased expenditures will be immediately infused into some service areas, while having a delayed impact in others.

The nature and level of service impacts depends, to a large extent, on the number of immigrants entering in a period. Large immigration influxes are sometimes difficult to predict and difficult to budget. Emergency expenditures in one category of the municipal budget are expected to be counterbalanced by decreases in other components. The overall effect may be that some services experience a larger infusion of resources while others face declining resources. However, those service areas that were originally reduced will, over time, see additional resource flows to compensate for the history of declines.

To provide parsimony while discussing particular service areas, service types have been divided into direct and demand-responsive programs. Direct services are those activities which are established to fulfill a particular need, such as public safety or sanitation, and are typically managed directly by local governments. Further, these services are not tied to any particular consumer, and are available to all residents. They may be public goods, such as police and fire services, but they may also be toll goods such as sanitation, certain parks and recreation programs, or other such user-charge services.

Demand services, on the other hand, are programs which react to the needs of individuals and groups. Therefore, demand-responsive services may be impacted differently than directed services by immigrants. Immigrants may be unwilling to seek government assistance, although eligible, because they are unfamiliar with or hesitant to approach government institutions fearing some form of sanctions or reprisal (see Chapter 4).

In demand-responsive programs, governments cannot control the rate or type of demand, such as the number of individuals entering a particular school system or the number of individuals requiring food stamps or AFDC. Moreover, these services are typically not directly controlled by a local jurisdiction, and individuals must actively seek assistance from these programs. To complicate the isolation of demand-responsive service impacts, in most cases a municipality acts as a "pass-through" for state or federal resources and there may or may not be local matching requirements. We assume that most of the demand-responsive programs are not directly controlled by local jurisdictions and therefore are beyond the scope and intentions of this research effort.

Hypothesis 8: Departments with direct service responsibility—police, fire, solid waste, streets, water, and parks and recreation—will be impacted fairly early by immigrant arrivals. Specific services having a positive association with immigration include police services (throughout the first seven years after arrival), fire services (after the second year), sanitation (over the entire study period), and parks and recreation (with sharp peaks and valleys throughout the period). An interesting finding is that the specific impacts on police, fire, garbage, and parks and recreation are positive, but when all services are included, the overall association between immigration and the change in general government expenditures is negative shortly after arrival.

During the middle period of the lag (from three through five years after arrival), immigration is positively associated with the change in deflated expenditures for streets, sewers, police, and, to a limited extent, general government expenditures. Immigration is associated with expenditure increases six to eight years after arrival for fire service, sanitation, parks and recreation, and public-building management. The analysis suggests expenditures for police, sanitation, and parks feel the first impacts, and are followed by increased expenditures for streets, sewers, fire service, and general government.

Police Department

The results of the models suggest police expenditures increase at the year of entry ($13 per immigrant) and then continue to increase, peaking four years after entry (at $58 per immigrant). Over the entire period from year of entry through eight years after entry, immigration is associated with an increase in deflated per capita expenditures for police of about $300, or $369 in 1989 dollars (Table 5.6).

Streets Department

The streets department is responsible for the maintenance and repair of all city-owned streets. In addition, beautification projects, such as adding trees and flowers to medians, often fall under this expenditure category. This program area is significantly different than police expenditures in that immigration pressures may be delayed as a local government begins to sort out impacts. The distributed-lag model predicting change in deflated expenditures for the streets department associates immigration with small decreases the year of entry and the next two years (decreases of $12 the year of entry, $10 the next year, and less then a $1 per immigrant the second year after entry). This is followed by steadily larger increases in streets expenditures, peaking six years after entry but continuing through the eighth year (increases of $15 per immigrant the third year, $32 the fourth, $47 the fifth,

Table 5.6
Expenditures by Selected Service Area Starting in Year of Arrival

Year	Police	Fire	Sanitation	Parks and Recreation	Streets	Finance
0	$ 13.29	$-30.62	$ 0.68	$ 208.86	$-11.61	$-31.49
1	28.03	-17.97	2.99	119.48	-10.45	27.12
2	41.98	7.06	6.30	-42.94	0.27	-10.64
3	52.92	24.57	9.94	-134.98	15.17	2.10
4	58.62	25.66	13.27	-94.99	32.12	3.22
5	56.86	12.43	15.62	56.92	46.83	-7.25
6	45.41	-2.04	16.35	218.85	55.53	21.32
7	22.04	6.34	14.81	207.16	54.48	23.07
8	-15.47	72.65	10.33	-243.60	39.92	11.36
Total	$303.68	$ 98.08	$90.29	$ 294.76	$222.26	$ 38.81

$56 the sixth, $54 the seventh, and $40 per immigrant the eighth year after entry).

In contrast to the original hypothesis, immigration is associated with a net increase in streets expenditures (deflated) by the fourth year after entry, and is associated with an overall increase in deflated expenditures for streets of about $220 ($270 in 1989 dollars) per immigrant. A major reason for this finding is that the increased pressure on infrastructure placed by immigrants (i.e., population pressure) forces local governments to eventually increase expenditures, because streets have been neglected for so long that repairs need to be accomplished. This lends support to the discussion of capital-expenditure increases in the preceding section. Another line of argument is that once the direct-service requirements begin to stabilize, additional resources are spent on these categories.

Fire Services

When evaluating the impact of different variables on public safety expenditures, many researchers often assume that the relationship between police and fire services is similar. It is assumed for this analysis that, in fact, they are substantially different. The model examining the response of fire-service expenditures as a result of immigration indicates an initial period of expenditure decline (a decrease of $30 per immigrant the year of entry and $18 the next year), followed by a series of small increases ($7 increase the second year after entry, $25 the third, $26 the fourth, and $12 the fifth) which, by the fourth year after entry, have made up for the initial decline. After two years of stable expenditures, immigration is associated with a fairly large increase ($73 per immigrant) eight years after entry. Over the entire period, the model estimates that immigration leads to a net increase in fire-service expenditures of $98 ($119 in 1989 dollars), mostly occurring the eighth year after entry. Thus, fire-service expenditures increase by about 30 percent of the amount found for police expenditures.

Consistent with the original assumptions, fire expenditures show a marked decrease the year of arrival, followed by a modest decline the next year. After the second year, immigrants are associated with a small increase in expenditures. These increases are presumably a result of poor funding habits of previous years, or the fact that fire-service expenditures respond slowly to increased population pressures. In either case, over the long term, immigration is associated positively with expenditures in this area.

Sanitation (Garbage and Trash)

As a consumption-based service, the impact of immigration on sanitation expenditures will be quick; typically the first year of arrival. However, long-term expenditures may only be marginally impacted, since other program areas will receive additional resources at the expense of sanitation expenditures. Moreover, when immigrants become settled in the community, move out on their own, or become employed, their consumption habits change. Further, many of these individuals may have originated from a country in which recycling was not promoted, but, feeling the pressure to recycle, actually generate less garbage.

Results indicate that, in the year of arrival, immigrants only increase sanitation expenses by $1 per immigrant. The impact peaks six years after arrival, when immigrants increase sanitation expenses by $16. Over the eight-year time horizon, immigrants generate around $90 ($109 in 1989 dollars) in additional expenditures for this service.

Sewers

As a population-sensitive service, it is assumed that the additional expenditure pressures brought on by immigrants will impact sewer expenditures very early. This may be mitigated to some degree if the influx of immigration is spread over a period of years. The addition of one individual should not tax facilities to the point where large capital expenditures are required to maintain the system. However, when a large number of immigrants enter in a brief period, or over a couple of years, the pressures for additional facilities may show up in large capital expenditures.

The model predicting changes in Miami's deflated expenditures on sewers (a third-degree polynomial) indicates initial small increases (increases estimated at about $14 per immigrant during the year of entry, $13 the following year, $5 two years after entry), followed by a four-year period of small decreases that tend to cancel out the initial increases (decreases of $6,

$15, $15, and $1 per immigrant), and ending with two relatively large increases ($33 per immigrant the seventh year after entry and $91 the eighth). The net effect of immigration on deflated sewer expenditures is, according to the analysis, an increase of about $120 ($145 in 1989 dollars) per immigrant, but this comes at the end of the study period, seven and eight years after entry.

Parks and Recreation

When confronted with increased service demands caused by immigrants, parks and recreation expenditures should increase. As more individuals use these services, such as visiting local parks, using facilities, or consuming other activities, expenses increase. Most of the increases can be buffeted to a degree, in that an additional consumer may not overly tax the facility. However, during high levels of immigration, program expenses can be expected to rise. During incremental immigration, expenditures can be expected to rise only marginally.

The estimated model predicting deflated parks and recreation expenditures is volatile. Sharp increases the year of entry ($209 per immigrant) and the first year after entry ($119) are followed by relatively sharp decreases the next three years that nearly cancel out the early increases (decreases of $43, $134, and $94 per immigrant). The fifth, sixth, and seventh years after entry are again characterized by large increases ($57, $219, and $207 per immigrant) and the eighth year by a large decrease ($243 per immigrant).

Overall, the model's estimate of immigration's effect on parks and recreation is a net increase of nearly $300 ($358 in 1989 dollars) per immigrant. The relatively large, albeit erratic, effect on parks reflects, in part, the City of Miami's use of parks as temporary shelters and processing points for arriving immigrants.

Financial Administration

As an internal administrative function, like personnel, city management, and similar activities, it is assumed that as local governments face limited resource capacity finance will fall victim to budgetary cuts. The finance department, as a reflection of other similar administrative activities, will bear an undue burden of immigrations impact. When policy makers are confronted with reductions, they prefer to cut where there is little external support for programs. Very infrequently do citizens request additional resources for financial activities of the city, but many staunchly protest cuts in other areas like police. Therefore, the finance department will initially feel the financial impact of immigration.

Empirical results indicate that immigration is associated with three years of decreases in deflated financial administration expenditures, followed by two years of small increases, three more years of decreases, and an increase in the final year (the eighth after entry). The net decrease associated with immigration in financial administration expenditures totals more then $100 ($126 in 1989 dollars) per immigrant.

As stated, core functions of the city, such as finance, personnel, and other administrative functions, were reduced throughout the time horizon of the study. These findings seem rather obvious, but results demonstrate the severity of the impacts. For every immigrant, there is an associated decline in financial expenditures by approximately $300 over eight years. Positive effects are found in only two periods: between the fourth and fifth years, and during the eighth year.

General Government Expenditures

General government expenditures are not for specific programmatic areas or personnel, but are expenditures made by the municipality which have not been identified with specific department or functional categories. Some of the more common expenditures in this area include rent and royalties, contingency funds, auditor fees, outside legal council, and other such miscellaneous expenditures. Given the nature of this category, immigration is expected to have an overall negative effect. More specifically, throughout the time horizon of the study, expenditures for this area are expected to decline, but on occasion there may be a one-time increase as a result of economic pressures.

The distributed-lag model predicting deflated general government expenditures associates immigration with a net decline in this expenditure category. The model indicates decreases in general government expenditures the year of entry and the next four years (decreases of $16, $21, $19, $13, and $5 per immigrant, respectively), followed by two years of small increases ($1 the fifth year and $2 the sixth), and then two more years of decreases ($4 and $21 per immigrant). The model estimates immigration's overall effect on deflated general government expenditures during the year of entry and the next eight years as a decrease of nearly $100 ($117 in 1989 dollars) per immigrant.

Total Expenditures

Employing the same analysis used for estimating revenue impacts, the bivariate correlation indicates Miami's immigration (documented and estimated total immigration) is associated with an increase in deflated general expenditures for the year following entry and further increases in deflated general expenditures for four through seven years after entry.

There is little apparent association between the year of arrival and the second and third years after arrival. The distributed-lag model, a third-degree polynomial, only explains about 9 percent of the variance in deflated general expenditures. It associates immigration in a given year with small decreases in general expenditures during the year of entry ($42 per immigrant) and the following year ($24), and increases in general expenditures for each of the next seven years, with the largest increase ($272) occurring in the sixth year after entry. The net increase in deflated general expenditures for the year of entry and the next eight years is estimated to be $1145 ($1391 in 1989 dollars) per immigrant.

COMPARING REVENUE AND EXPENDITURE PATTERNS

The general effects in the Miami case study during the 1980s are interesting. Concerning revenues, the effects of the 1980 Mariel influx show up in general revenue levels, but the impact is spread across many years (see Table 5.3). Immigration is associated with consistently positive increases in revenue, but the increases are the smallest during 1980 and 1981 ($8.1 and $8.7 million, respectively), the years during and after the Mariel influx. The revenue increases associated with immigration peak in 1984, when immigration is associated with an increase of $34 million in City of Miami revenues.

Immigration is associated with decreases in property tax revenues every year of the decade, and the decreases are largest during the three years after the Mariel influx and then again toward the end of the decade during a Central American influx. Immigration is associated with increases in sales tax revenues during most of the decade, but the increases are minor during the mid-1980s. Immigration has the largest effect on intergovernment revenue (IG), but the majority of the impact came in the mid-1980s during the Reagan era, well after the Mariel influx and well before the Central American influx.

Conversely, the effect of immigration on expenditures is stable across the decade (Table 5.7). The lag tends to moderate the impact of even the large Mariel influx. General-expenditure increases peak in 1985 and 1986 (increases of $31.1 and $31.4 million), after the Mariel influx, and are smallest in 1989 (an increase of $15.9 million) during the Central American influx.

A rough measure of the fiscal impact of immigration is provided by the difference between lagged revenue and expenditure figures. Revenue increases associated with immigration are generally smaller then expenditure increases. In the early 1980s, during and immediately after the Mariel influx, the discrepancy between revenue and expenditure is at its largest. In 1980, immigration is associated with an increase of $24.8 million in general expenditures and only $8.1 million in revenues, a discrepancy of over $16 million. During 1983 and 1984, the revenue increases associated with immigration exceed expenditure increases, but by less then $6 million each

Table 5.7
Yearly Change in City of Miami Expenditures Attributable to Immigration (Millions of 1989 Dollars)

Service	Year										
	79	80	81	82	83	84	85	86	87	88	89
General	29.6	24.8	24.0	24.5	25.5	28.4	31.1	31.4	28.7	21.9	15.9
Personnel	17.4	18.7	19.6	19.8	19.2	18.4	17.6	16.4	15.1	14.0	12.9
Capital	17.3	13.8	13.0	13.9	13.2	14.0	16.0	17.1	17.3	15.8	8.5
Police	6.4	6.8	7.1	7.0	7.4	7.7	7.4	6.8	5.5	3.7	4.8
Sanitation	2.2	2.0	2.0	2.1	2.0	2.1	2.2	2.2	2.1	1.8	1.3
Streets	6.1	4.8	4.6	4.8	4.8	5.3	6.0	6.3	6.1	5.1	3.0
Fire	3.6	0.8	0.8	3.4	3.7	3.0	2.2	1.3	1.8	4.9	1.3
Sewer	3.7	3.4	3.3	4.1	2.4	1.0	1.2	1.9	3.8	6.7	2.0
Parks	2.3	17.8	16.1	-0.4	-5.7	-0.6	7.5	17.0	15.5	-6.2	5.0
General Government	-2.1	-2.5	-2.7	-2.9	-2.3	-1.6	-1.3	-1.3	-1.7	-2.7	-1.7
Financial Admin.	-1.8	-3.6	-3.6	-2.2	-1.3	-1.3	-1.9	-2.7	-2.8	-1.3	-1.8
Public Building	0.7	0.5	0.4	0.4	0.5	0.6	0.7	0.7	0.6	0.5	0.3

year. Therefore, the relationship to immigration is stronger for expenditures than for revenues within the study period, and the overall fiscal association is negative.

As Figure 5.1 indicates, there is only one period when immigrants generate more general fund revenues than they consume in local services. This occurs during the second through fifth years after arrival. There are many reasons which explain this occurrence, but this increase is primarily due to the fact that, as immigrants are employed, their contributions to the public coffers increase at a faster rate than their consumption of local government services. During their first two years, they consume more services than they generate through tax revenues. However, as immigrants become settled in a community over time, their demands for services increase at a faster rate than their contributions as, some have argued, they start imitating native practices.

The overall findings suggest that throughout the eight-year time horizon of the study, each immigrant produces a net negative impact on local government of $225.58. This figure represents an annualized cost of roughly

Figure 5.1
Changes in Revenues and Expenditures over an Eight-Year Span

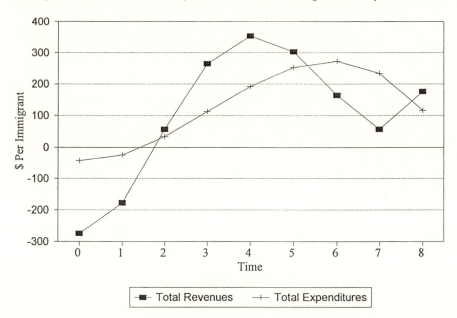

$25. Therefore, based on the general findings, immigration into a community is a financial burden to the municipality. However, as Figure 5.1 indicates, in the eighth year immigrants again begin to produce more revenues than they consume in services. This may or may not continue into the future, and can only be validated through further study. The estimation of specific expenditures and revenues is needed to understand their overall relationship. This more detailed analysis is guided by the working hypotheses derived from the results of the Delphi survey and supported by earlier research.

SUMMARY

Identifying and isolating the fiscal impact immigrants have on municipal revenues and expenditures is complicated by many factors, such as the ebbs and flows of legal and illegal migration or relating revenue and expenditure patterns specifically to immigration flows. To handle these limitations, multiple methods were used to expose potential impacts and evaluate those impacts empirically. The methods suggested do not lend full support to the contention that immigrants positively or negatively impact local government finances. Findings from the Miami case study indicate that, over an eight-year time horizon, immigrants cost a municipal organization roughly $226 or $25 per annum (Table 5.8). The limitations of this research and previous efforts must be considered in attempting to relate specific local government revenue and expenditure decisions to immigration. That is, stating that immigrants cost a local government "X" amount of dollars presupposes that all revenue and expenditure sources were analyzed and that a determination was made that immigrants use these sources in a substantially different way from current residents. However, an alternate explanation is that immigrants consume roughly the same amount of resources as current residents, but have become the scapegoat for general fiscal decline in a city, as evidenced by the recent voter approval of Proposition 187 in California.

The methods employed to study the impact of immigration on municipal revenues and expenditures—bivariate correlational analysis and a polynomial distributed-lag technique—exposed certain characteristics that, although not statistically significant across all sources, demonstrated substantially important fiscal impacts. While the methods utilized do not allow for causal inferences, such as stating that immigration alone accounts for declines in property tax revenues received during a given year, they do offer policy makers a broader understanding of the potential impacts of immigration on revenues and expenditures.

From the analysis conducted for the City of Miami, findings indicate that immigrants have the strongest impact on specific revenues and expenditures,

Table 5.8
Comparative Fiscal Impact of Immigration Revenues and Expenditures Starting in Year of Arrival

Year	Total General Government Revenue	Total General Government Expenditure	Difference
0	$ −274.30	$ −42.17	$ −232.13
1	−177.37	−24.20	−153.17
2	56.42	34.02	22.40
3	263.83	112.63	151.20
4	352.82	191.74	161.08
5	302.55	251.49	51.06
6	163.32	272.00	−108.68
7	56.64	233.39	−176.75
8	175.19	115.78	59.41
Total	$ 919.10	$ 1144.68	$ −225.58

and that, over the time horizon of the study, the impact has been negative. Given the magnitude of the impact ($225.58 per immigrant) over the eight years, this may be construed as an insignificant finding. That is, given the various limitations of the methods, data, time, and differentiating fiscal relationships, findings may not be overly important. If each immigrant only costs municipalities roughly $25 a year more than each native, is this an unfair burden? In contrast, if this estimate is overly conservative, and immigrants cost municipalities substantially more, the issue becomes how much more and what avenues are available that local administrators can pursue to ameliorate these impacts.

A final area that municipal administrators need to be able to address is the likely future levels of immigration their community will face. Chapter 6 provides a working example for making a municipal-based empirical forecast of immigration levels.

NOTES

1. In our case study, local and state criminal justice agencies collected the best statistics on involvement with immigrants through data on criminal suspects, especially since the Mariel influx. However, data on arrested immigrants address very limited aspects of immigration's effects; sometimes simply immigration's effects on police services.

2. Unless otherwise noted, expenditures and revenues are presented in constant dollars rather than current dollars. This was necessary to analyze interyear differences, as well as to compare trends over time.

3. The eight-year lag was selected based on the time frame of historical information. It is given that as more years are added to the data base, the lag can be extended.

4. Hypotheses which guide the development and interpretation of empirical results were generated from two sources: (1) extensive literature review and (2) the authors' assumptions about anticipated relationships between immigration and revenue and expenditure decisions exposed in the Delphi survey.

5. Tables with the results of the distributed-lag model are voluminous, and those interested in exploring these data should see Loveless et al., 1990.

6. Second-, third-, and fourth-degree Almon polynomial models were analyzed for each of the financial variables. The fit of the models were evaluated based on variance explained, Akaikis information criteria, SBC, and interpretability. Strong preference was given to models fixing the impact of immigration on previous years' revenues or expenditures at zero and, all other factors being equal, preference is given to parsimonious models (i.e., models estimated with third- rather than fourth-degree polynomials).

Generally, the pattern of lagged coefficients was similar across various models, though the particular model chosen does have an impact on the absolute magnitude of the coefficient. Consequently, specific coefficients should be treated with some skepticism. Four- and six-year lag models were estimated in addition to the eight-year period used for the final estimates. The eight-year period was chosen based on the lengthy lag period seen in the bivariate analysis.

7. Examination of the Durbin–Watson statistic for the various lag models indicated that autocorrelation was not a problem. Although time-series data are employed, the use of the change (first differences) in expenditures and per capita expenditures mitigates the problem of autocorrelation.

8. It is difficult to explain the initial decline in revenue. The loss may well be due to other demographic and financial factors than immigration, but the loss does suggest that Miami has had to cope with declines in deflated revenues at the same time as it was coping with larger than usual immigration flows.

CHAPTER 6

Immigration Forecasts

A primary function of effective public management is to anticipate events and develop current means for dealing with their potentialities. Therefore, forecasting the level of future immigration and the likelihood of utilization of government services by the predicted immigrant groups becomes a very critical part of the local government managerial process. This chapter deals with an important component of analyzing the impact of immigration on municipal resources—forecasting future immigration. There are many limitations to forecasting immigration and analyzing its financial impact. However, the use of both qualitative and quantitative methods increases the reliability and validity of forecasting results.

Within the confines of analysis, decision makers should be cognizant that any forecast is simply a projection of future outcomes based on perceptions of alternative futures. Consequentially, results should be evaluated within the limitations of the data and techniques. The methods proposed herein provide a baseline for anticipating immigration flows and developing operating policies to ameliorate impacts. Like any form of forecasting, however, the results should be buffered by a range of alternative futures that anticipate both high and low levels. This is particularly necessary given the highly idiosyncratic nature of international migration and the multiple levels of immigration effects on public programs throughout the United States.

The Delphi survey technique discussed in Chapter 4 was utilized to collect one set of data employed in forecasting. The Delphi used the responses of national and local experts to predict the impact of immigration, as well as future levels of immigration. Forecasts can also be estimated through statistical modeling. Projections of this nature are based, in part, on past immigration flows and their potential for existence in the future. The accuracy of these forecasts are predicated on the assumption that "trends" will continue in the future as they did in the past. Although these assumptions are often violated, statistical models provide useful tools to bound future immigration levels. This is most relevant when findings are combined with results of judgmental forecasting techniques, like the Delphi results.

In this chapter, several quantitative forecasting techniques are used to model archival data and predict immigration over the 1990s. In that these estimates were completed on pre-1989 and 1990 data sets, the 1989 forecasts for Miami can be compared with the actual 1989 immigration to Miami, providing a unique validity test and comparison for the various forecast techniques. To demonstrate the various techniques, separate estimates of documented, undocumented, and total immigration are developed for the City of Miami. At the end of the chapter, recent events affecting immigration are summarized, and an evaluation is rendered regarding the efficacy of both qualitative and quantitative methodologies for local government administrators.

QUANTITATIVE IMMIGRATION FORECASTING

Employing the parameters established by the Delphi-survey findings, various statistical techniques are used to forecast yearly and aggregate immigration levels to the year 2000. As previously noted, statistical forecasts are based on the assumption that the past is prologue to future immigration flows. Several dynamic elements of immigration suggest past trends may be quite useful in predicting future levels. For example, the Delphi and field-survey analyses used in the City of Miami study support previous research suggesting that immigrants are drawn to areas with an established immigrant community. They learn about a particular community from fellow countrymen who have already immigrated to that area. They anticipate assistance and support from established immigrants and fewer problems with language, employment, and socialization. In addition, undocumented aliens find anonymity and, hence, safety from discovery and deportation in areas where large numbers of fellow countrymen reside.

The past becomes prologue more directly with the large number of documented immigrants who arrive through first-preference status for family reunification, granted under the Immigration and Nationalization Act (INA) of 1990. As has been noted, over 90 percent of documented immigrants arrive with visa classifications based, at least in part, on having family members in the United States. The expansion and first-preference status of family-status visas granted under INA of 1990 adds momentum to family reunification as a primary determinant of future immigration flows.

In contrast to factors suggesting that past immigration levels help predict future levels, abrupt shifts in immigration flows documented throughout history (and the difficulties of getting an accurate count of immigrants residing in a particular municipality) limit the reliability of statistically generated forecasts. The enumeration problems have been discussed at length in Chapter 2. The difficulties of counting undocumented immigrants, tracking movements by immigrants (documented and undocumented) within the United States after entry, and estimating the number of immigrants who return to their home country are only three of the more severe constraints to an accurate enumeration. Further complicating the analysis is the paucity of longitudinal data points. Statistics on documented immigration for most municipalities have only been available since the early 1980s, not nearly long enough to develop reliable quantitative forecasts.

Even if there was a method of insuring perfectly reliable archival data, forecasting immigration's financial impact would be very difficult. The frequent and unpredictable radical shifts in immigration flow reflect the volatility of international political and economic dislocations. These shifts destroy the series stability that trend analysis relies on. Therefore, qualitative predictions must be used to supplement statistical techniques to develop useable forecasting models. The statistical forecasts provide estimations that, taken together or sensitized with expert opinion, generate more accurate assessments of possible immigration futures.

Unfortunately, no statistical or qualitative method can predict with certainty specific levels during specific times. Both techniques utilized in the model should be used as a planning tool for anticipating and dealing with the many difficulties associated with immigration projections. The technique's strength is most valuable when immigration levels are part idiosyncratic and part constant. The large-scale immigration waves that experts participating in the Delphi survey were so hesitant to predict make any statistical forecast prone to large errors. However, when baseline projections are used as a guide in managing immigration flows, the methods may potentially forestall many of the problems of simply not anticipating immigration.

FORECAST MODELS AND RESULTS

Forecast models that predict future immigration based on past levels have been developed for the City of Miami. The derivation of the archival immigration data used in developing the forecasts is discussed in Chapter 2. Separate forecasts were developed for (1) total immigration (documented and undocumented combined) calculated using Warren and Passel's adjustment ratio discussed in Chapter 3; (2) total immigration including the school-based estimate of undocumented immigration; (3) total documented immigration for both documented new arrivals and adjustment immigrants; (4) current immigration focusing on new arrivals; (5) undocumented immigration estimated using Warren and Passel's proportional-adjustment figures; and (6) undocumented immigration using the school-based technique.

Where sufficient data exist, three different techniques were used to develop forecasts: exponential smoothing, autoregression, and ARIMA. Each technique is a derivative of the trend analysis often used in forecasting. The techniques assume that the future is linked empirically to the past. However, there are no assumptions made linking certain independent variables to immigration flows. Although these more "sophisticated" techniques are promoted as more precise than relying on more judgmental and trend-based forecasts, the literature on the level of accuracy when comparing more methodologically advanced techniques to simple techniques has been mixed. In fact, many current scholars in the forecasting field argue that simple techniques are as accurate in the short run as more statistically advanced techniques (Armstrong, 1985; Mentzer and Cox, 1984).

Methodology

The forecasting techniques utilized in the Miami study are briefly highlighted in the following section. The primary assumptions of the methods employed are that there are discernable trends in immigration and that the various techniques can isolate those trends and project them forward. There are two critical components of these assumptions. The first is linearity. Since the exponential-smoothing and ARIMA techniques make the assumption that a line can be detected to represent future patterns, if this assumption is violated (i.e., the relationship is curvilinear), the techniques will fail to capture these movements.

The second assumption of the techniques is that the sudden and erratic shifts in immigration have some consistent pattern. This assumption has already been violated in the Miami case study. Nevertheless, the techniques can isolate underlying trends, even given the idiosyncratic nature of the shifts. The weakness of using these methods is that the error around the prediction may be so large that the figures presented appear faulty. For example, as exhibited in the Miami study, the lower boundaries of the models may predict negative immigration. In reality, this certainly cannot be the case. In situations where the confidence intervals fall below 0, one would suspect that the line is truly not accurate.

If results indicate a large confidence interval around the point estimate, one should not abandon the figures because we cannot be confident at a given level that immigration will be within a range. A large confidence interval simply implies that, in order to be 95-percent confident that immigration will fall within a certain range, a wide interval is needed. On the other hand, the estimates do offer a baseline of potential immigration, providing valuable planning and management information.

City of Miami Findings

Past immigration to Miami makes statistical forecasts of total documented and combined documented and undocumented immigration difficult.[1] Major shifts in immigration occur with little apparent pattern. However, this is where the impact of limited historical information is felt. If sufficient longitudinal data were available, peaks and valleys in the immigration cycle could be extrapolated. Unfortunately, data constraints do not allow for such analysis. Therefore, the validity of results should be considered within the limitations of the data.

Total Documented Immigration. As Table 6.1 indicates, the two "best fit" ARIMA models[2] estimate 1990 documented immigration at between –18,881 and 26,300 (best guess of 3,884) and between –9,975 and 33,828 (best guess of 9,521), respectively. The estimates for the year 2000 are even farther apart, with the first model predicting a decrease between –30,799 and 34,722 (best guess of 1,962), and the second model an increase between –8,594 and 35,887 (best guess of 13,647) documented immigrant arrivals.

Both the exponential-smoothing[3] and autoregressive[4] forecasts predict declines in documented immigrants arriving in Miami, but the confidence intervals for these forecasts are very wide. The exponential-smoothing

Table 6.1
City of Miami Immigration Forecasts: Documented Immigration (Thousands of Immigrants)

	1990			2000			1990–2000		
	High	Mid	Low	High	Mid	Low	High	Mid	Low
TOTAL DOCUMENTED									
ARIMA (0,1,1)	26.3	3.9	–18.9	34.7	2.0	–30.8	338.7	31.2	–276.3
ARIMA (1,0,0)	33.8	9.5	–10.0	35.9	13.6	–8.6	391.4	147.2	–97.1
Exponential Smoothing	30.5	3.4	–23.5	28.5	–5.0	–38.4	321.5	–6.7	–335.0
Auto Regression	28.8	6.6	–15.6	26.1	2.5	–21.2	301.5	49.8	–201.9
NEW-ARRIVAL DOCUMENTED									
Exponential Smoothing	4.7	2.9	1.1	5.3	3.0	0.8	54.6	32.6	10.6

Note: The new arrival series was too short and too unstable to estimate with ARIMA or autoregressive models model estimates 1990 documented immigration at between –23,599 and 30,458 (best guess of 3,429), and Miami's documented immigration in the year 2000 at between –38,440 and 28,511 (best guess of –4,965). The autoregressive forecast estimates 1990 documented immigration at between –15,598 and 28,794 (best guess of 6,598), and documented immigration in the year 2000 at between –21,183 and 26,112 (best guess of 2,465). These estimates are too imprecise to be of much use to policy makers or administrators. The underlying series is characterized by too much instability to yield useful forecasts.

The width of the confidence interval around these estimates is highlighted when the yearly estimates are summed for a total 1990 to 2000 forecast. The most likely projections for the decade range from the exponential-smoothing projection of –6,700 to the one-lag ARIMA projection of 147,200 documented immigrants over this period.

New Arrival Documented Immigration. When the adjustment immigrants are removed from the series, it is easier to forecast documented immigration (see Table 6.1).[5] The exponential-smoothing model predicts between 1,100 and 4,700 (best guess of 2,900) new arrival immigrants for 1990, and between 800 and 5,300 (best guess of 3,000) are estimated for the year 2000. Over the entire decade, between 10,600 and 54,600 (best guess of 32,600) new arrival immigrants are expected to settle in Miami.

Total Immigration (Census Estimate). Estimates of total immigration include adjustment immigrants and are characterized by high margins of error and, therefore, are of marginal utility. The best fit ARIMA model for the estimate, incorporating census-based figures for undocumented immigration (a one-lag autoregressive model), estimates 1990 immigration at between –5,910 and 40,593 (with a best guess of 17,342), and total immigration in the year 2000 at between –5,685 and 40,831 (with a best guess of 17,573). The exponential-smoothing and autoregressive models, on the other hand, predict declining total immigration (see Table 6.2). The exponential model produces 1990 estimates bounded on the low end at –21,419 and on the high end at 37,730 (best guess of 8,155), and an estimate for the year 2000 of between –35,916 and 37,343 (best guess of 714) immigrants. The autoregressive model estimates between –12,611 and 36,252 (best guess of 11,821) immigrants arrived in 1990, and predicts the arrival of between –17,793 and 34,932 (best guess of 8,569) immigrants in the year 2000.

When summed, the various forecast models of census-estimate total immigration predict best-guess levels ranging from 50,400 (exponential smoothing) to 192,900 (ARIMA) for the decade. All three forecast techniques yield confidence-interval estimates for the decade of from well below zero to about 450,000 immigrants.

Total Immigration (School Data Estimate). The forecast models of total immigration using undocumented estimates derived from school data provide

Table 6.2
City of Miami Immigration Forecasts: Total Immigration (Thousands of Immigrants)

	1990			2000			1990–2000		
	High	Mid	Low	High	Mid	Low	High	Mid	Low
SCHOOL DATA ESTIMATE									
ARIMA	44.4	21.1	-2.2	45.0	21.4	-2.2	494.0	234.7	-24.7
Exponential Smoothing	44.7	14.4	-15.9	46.0	14.4	-15.9	495.2	127.3	-240.7
Auto Regression	42.0	17.1	-12.5	40.8	14.1	-12.5	454.4	170.7	-113.0
CENSUS DATA ESTIMATE									
ARIMA	40.6	17.3	-5.9	40.8	17.6	-5.7	448.8	192.9	-62.9
Exponential Smoothing	37.7	8.2	-21.4	37.3	1.0	-35.9	409.6	50.4	-308.8
Auto Regression	36.3	11.8	-12.6	34.9	8.6	-17.8	391.0	112.1	-166.7

Note: Includes documented and undocumented immigrants.

higher estimates with equally large margins of error. The best ARIMA model (using a single autoregressive lag) estimates total immigration in 1990 at between –2,212 and 44,402, with a best guess estimate of 21,094 immigrants. The model predicts the level of immigration in the year 2000 to be between –2,236 and 44,985, with a best guess of 21,375 immigrants (see Table 6.2). The exponential-smoothing model estimates 1990 total immigration at between –15,928 and 44,670, with a best guess of 14,371 immigrants. Immigration in the year 2000 is estimated at between –29,020 and 46,033, with a best guess of 8,506 immigrants. The autoregressive model estimates between –7,774 and 41,974 immigrants arrived in Miami during 1990 (with a best guess estimate of 17,100), and that between –12,541 and 40,809 immigrants will arrive in Miami in the year 2000 (with a best guess estimate of 14,134 immigrants).

Summed across the decade, the best guesses of the various estimation techniques range from 127,300 (exponential smoothing) to 234,700 (ARIMA) immigrants. The confidence-interval limits for all three forecasting techniques yield decade-total low estimates below zero and high estimates close to 500,000 immigrants. Although the range is rather broad, they do provide for contingency planning on behalf of local administrators.

Undocumented Immigration (Census Data Estimate). The estimates of undocumented immigration derived from the more conservative census-based data are, as expected, lower. The best ARIMA model, a model made up of a single moving average parameter, estimates the number of undocumented immigrants for both 1990 and the year 2000 to be between 1,209 and 5,214 with a best guess of 3,212 (see Table 6.3). The exponential-smoothing model estimates between 563 and 5,804 (with a best guess of 3,184) undocumented immigrants arrived in Miami in 1990, and that between –247 and 6,245 (best guess of 2,999) undocumented immigrants will arrive with the intention of residing in the City of Miami for the year 2000.

The autoregressive model suggests as few as 1,164 and as many as 5,423 (best guess of 3,293) undocumented immigrants arrived in Miami in 1990, and predicts that between 1,497 and 6,124 (best guess of 3,810) undocumented immigrants will arrive in the year 2000.

Summed across the decade, the three techniques yield quite similar projections. The decade-long best guess estimates range from 34,100 to 40,200 undocumented immigrants. The total of the low ends of the confidence intervals range from 2,300 to 15,600 and the high ends total from 57,400 to 65,900 immigrants.

Undocumented Immigration (School Data Estimate). Estimates of undocumented immigration (adjustment immigrants are not included in these estimates) have a smaller range then total documented immigration and total immigration.[6] The best-fit ARIMA model for the school-based estimate of undocumented immigration (a one-lag autoregressive model) estimates 1990

Table 6.3
City of Miami Immigration Forecasts: Estimated Undocumented Immigration (Thousands of Immigrants)

	1990			2000			1990–2000		
	High	Mid	Low	High	Mid	Low	High	Mid	Low
SCHOOL DATA ESTIMATE									
ARIMA	14.0	9.5	5.0	13.1	7.7	2.3	147.1	88.7	30.2
Exponential Smoothing	16.9	11.0	5.0	20.9	13.6	6.2	206.8	134.8	62.8
Auto Regression	15.1	10.6	6.1	16.9	11.8	6.7	176.2	122.2	68.3
CENSUS DATA ESTIMATE									
ARIMA	5.2	3.2	1.2	5.2	3.2	1.2	57.4	35.3	13.3
Exponential Smoothing	5.8	3.2	0.6	6.2	3.0	-0.2	65.9	34.1	2.3
Auto Regression	5.4	3.3	1.2	6.1	3.8	1.5	64.8	40.2	15.6

undocumented immigration at between 5,027 and 14,012 (best guess of 9,519), and undocumented immigration in the year 2000 at between 2,250 and 13,121 (best guess of 7,685; see Table 6.3). The exponential-smoothing model estimates 1990 undocumented immigration at between 5,005 and 16,923, with a best guess estimate of 10,994, and by the year 2000 predicts yearly undocumented immigration to rise slightly to between 6,221 and 20,908, with a best guess estimate of 13,565. The autoregressive model estimate for 1990 is between 6,121 and 15,112 (best guess of 10,616) undocumented immigrants, and for the year 2000 is between 6,723 and 16,907 (best guess of 11,815) undocumented immigrants.

The sum total of forecasted best guesses for the decade ranges from 88,700 (ARIMA) to 134,800 (exponential smoothing) undocumented immigrants. The decade-long lower limits range from 30,200 to 68,300 and the upper limits range from 147,100 to 206,800 undocumented immigrants. These estimates are a little more useful to managers but the prospect of making policy decisions based on knowing that between 30,200 and 206,800 undocumented immigrants can be expected to arrive over the next ten years is daunting. This severe limitation is compounded when alternative methods of calculating archival levels are factored in with undocumented aliens.

DISCUSSION

The statistical forecasts are of limited utility, at least as long-term forecasts of actual immigration levels (Table 6.4). Total immigration and total documented immigration forecasts are characterized by extremely large confidence intervals which produce high levels of uncertainty. The uncertainty

Table 6.4
Comparison of Statistical Forecasts to Actual Documented Immigration: 1989

	High	Mid	Low	Actual
ARIMA (0,1,1)	26,300	3,900	−18,900	37,677
ARIMA (1,0,0)	33,800	9,500	−10,000	37,677
Exponential Smoothing	30,500	3,400	−23,500	37,677
Auto Regression	28,800	6,600	−15,600	37,677

in these forecasts reflects the instability of the underlying series, and the instability is largely a function of the adjustment portion of documented immigration. Adjustments in status include any immigrant who arrives with nonimmigrant status (sometimes illegally) and subsequently adjusts to immigrant status. In the Miami study, this category and, more important, the large shifts in this category, have been dominated by refugees and asylees. Forecasts of series excluding adjustments, new arrivals, and undocumented immigration are more precise and stable. However, given the uncertainties associated with estimating undocumented immigration, the precision may be illusionary. Unfortunately, it is the instability and sudden radical shifts that are most important for municipal governments to anticipate and plan for.

The forecasts are of greater utility as an indicator of uncertainty. The field survey and Delphi results suggest the importance of contingency planning for major influxes, and they provide an indication of the bounds of immigration that should be anticipated in developing contingency strategies. As such, it should be recognized that forecasts involving undocumented aliens, and forecasts of total immigration including undocumented aliens, are conservative. The census-based forecast is based on the accuracy of the 1980 census-derived estimate of undocumented immigration. The 1980 census has been found in validation studies to include about half of the 1980 undocumented population, suggesting that forecasts predicated on census estimates may well need to be doubled.

Estimates of undocumented aliens are based on public school records and may represent an undercount of 10 percent or more undocumented students. Moreover, in using the school data to estimate an undocumented component, assumptions are made that the proportion of students among undocumented arrivals in a given year is equivalent to the proportion among documented arrivals that year. Again, this is likely to be a conservative estimate if one assumes that undocumented immigrants have higher labor force participation than other groups, which may suggest a lower proportion of dependents.

Both the levels and ranges of the forecasts make the assumption that the structure of the underlying data series will not change in the future. In other words, the rules governing both documented and undocumented immigration will not shift in the near future. This is, of course, an assumption which will be, and already has been, violated to some extent. The Immigration Reform and Control Act of 1986, for example, adds employer sanctions to the mix. At this point, the effects of this act have not been fully incorporated in the forecasts. It may or may not lead to a reduction in undocumented immigration and an increase in status adjustments. In addition, the recent North American Free Trade Agreement (NAFTA) may potentially delay the flow of undocumented aliens into the United States, but the current belief is that the flow will not be drastically reduced. In either scenario, we can only speculate on outcomes in the near future.

In addition to these limitations, many of the Cuban–Haitian immigrants in Miami have already adjusted to permanent resident status under IRCA and are now eligible for naturalization. The bulk of other aliens granted amnesty under the 1986 Act will be eligible for citizenship starting in 1995. Once they are citizens, their immediate family members can immigrate with priority status. The City of Miami should see a substantial increase in family reunification immigration over the next ten years which is not captured in the statistical forecasts.

Recent court-induced changes in asylum hearings are another example of structural changes affecting (perhaps invalidating) past statistics as a basis for estimates of future levels. The U.S. government has agreed to eliminate foreign policy considerations and border control as factors in determining asylum requests. Instead, the federal government will simply evaluate each applicant's claim of having "a well-founded fear of persecution if returned" on its own merits. Prior to this policy change, an applicant's asylum application was much more likely to be approved if the applicant's home country was not a U.S. ally. The immediate consequences of the policy change included rehearing 150,000 Guatemalan and Salvadoran asylum cases, and potentially a large number of Cuban and Haitians who entered Miami in 1994. The change essentially reduces U.S. control over asylum levels, and opens the possibility of substantially increased levels of immigration from this source by the 1994 Cuban and Haitian influx. A court decision supporting class-action challenges of INS decisions increases the likelihood of procedural scrutiny in the future.

The recent radical political and economic changes in Eastern Europe, and the possibility of these changes spreading to Asia and the Western Hemisphere (particularly Cuba), may represent yet another fundamental structural change. Economic problems and political instability in Eastern Europe and other areas following reform, along with a loosening of mobility restrictions under NAFTA, could lead to a period of massive immigration. South Florida would be particularly affected by a spread of reform to the Western Hemisphere, and would also receive a share of an Eastern European influx.

At a more basic level, the underlying motivation for immigration may be shifting. Massey (1990) argues that the economic dislocations and uncertainties created by development are as important, or perhaps more important, as wage differential and poverty as inducements to immigration. Technological development carries with it improvements in communication and transportation systems, which increase the opportunity and motivation for immigration. Extending Massey's argument to current policies may lead many to argue that NAFTA will eventually result in higher levels of undocumented aliens entering the United States, because many of the vehicles for lawful entry may fall victim to changing sentiments.

Finally, current political and economic conditions throughout the world will continue to change the structure of immigration to the United States. Many analysts, including the Miami study's Delphi participants, have emphasized the importance of immigrant enclaves as magnets for additional immigrants. Once an immigrant community reaches a critical mass, the costs and risks of immigrating decline for fellow countrymen because earlier immigrants can provide assistance in obtaining employment, overcoming language barriers, finding housing, and so on. Moreover, the opportunities of immigrating will be disseminated more widely in the home country through the network connections of the enclave. The United States has seen the development of enclaves from nearly every Western Hemisphere country over the last thirty years, and this suggests steadily escalating immigration.

SUMMARY

The current ability to forecast immigration can be seen as a questionable enterprise. However, the best guess ranges coupled with local municipal knowledge do supply working parameters for contingency planning regarding projected impacts, at least in the short term. Chapter 7 discusses such projections and draws conclusions regarding the overall relationship between immigration and municipal fiscal position indicated in this study.

NOTES

1. The archival data for Miami has been adjusted prior to developing forecasting models to compensate for the 1983 change in INS geographic-locator information. Prior to 1983, Miami totals include immigrants from the Miami area as well as from the City of Miami proper. Based on declines between 1982 and 1983, it was estimated that 1982 statistics included 3,600 non-Miami new arrivals, and that the 1982 census-based estimates of undocumented immigrants included 1,250 non-Miami immigrants.

2. The best fit for ARIMA models is determined using AIC and SBC statistics, white-noise hypothesis tests of residual autocorrelations, width of the forecast confidence range, and significance of autoregressive and moving average parameters. The first model is differenced once and then estimated with a single moving average parameter, and the second has only a one-lag autoregressive parameter.

3. A quadratic-trend model with triple exponential smoothing is used for the reported exponential-smoothing forecasts.

4. The autoregressive forecast method employed fits a trend model and then uses a backwards-stepping selection process that eliminates insignificant autoregressive parameters to arrive at the model used for the forecast. Forecasts using both quadratic and linear initial-trend models were examined and, in virtually all cases, the linear-trend model produced the best estimate (narrowest confidence range and nonnegative point estimates).

5. Immigrants who adjust to immigrant status after entering the United States illegally or under a nonimmigrant classification (including refugees and asylees, among others) are dropped from this analysis to compensate for the limitations of documenting their residency. For more discussion, see Chapter 2.

6. Primarily because refugees and asylees who eventually adjust to documented status are omitted from the undocumented category.

CHAPTER 7

Immigration and Municipal Services: Interpreting Projected Impacts

This chapter examines the impact of recent and projected immigration on municipal revenues and expenditures and briefly summarizes and synthesizes the major findings from earlier chapters. The results of the earlier steps of the impact model, including the immigration estimates and projections, the distributed-lag impact models, the immigrant field survey, and the Delphi, are merged to project the impact of immigration on municipal revenues and expenditures to the year 2000.

The projections, however, must be taken as suggestive. The quality of the projections is dependent on the quality of the data used to formulate the projections. Earlier chapters note the many limitations and assumptions entailed in estimates of past immigration levels. These are magnified when the estimates are used to construct models of immigration effects and to predict future levels of immigration, and magnified again when combining immigration predictions with impact models to estimate future fiscal impacts. The point estimates of immigration impact provided in this chapter mask the margin of error characterizing the underlying data and impact-model parameters. In other words, the confidence intervals for the underlying individual components are very wide, and thus challenge the level of certainty in the point estimates.

One of the more severe problems is that, because of the minimal number of data points available, the impact analysis and projections lump together all immigrants, regardless of nationality or socioeconomic status. This ignores the fact (as demonstrated in the field survey and Delphi study) that the characteristics of a particular group of immigrants have an effect on their contribution to municipal revenues and public service consumption. Limiting individual demographic characteristics also ignores the fact that (as demonstrated in the archival analysis) the complexion of immigration and, thus, characteristics of immigrants, change over time. At this juncture, however, there are simply not enough usable data points available to incorporate changing patterns of immigrant characteristics into the projections. The failure to incorporate these shifts limits our ability to predict patterns in revenues and expenditures. In turn, this has the potential to bias estimates of future impacts by underestimating or overestimating those effects.

Moreover, statistically based projections are always founded on the assumption that past trends will continue, which, as noted in previous chapters, is a questionable assumption. Given that past trends are volatile, projections of financial effects on government and municipal planning should retain flexibility and resource slack to allow for sudden unexpected deviations from base immigration levels. This is especially important for host communities and those communities with preestablished immigrant enclaves. For the municipal administrator, the bottom line is that local, idiosyncratic knowledge is irreplaceable in assessing forecasts and formulating contingency plans.

Given the sizable list of caveats, why develop statistical impact projections? Two factors increase confidence in the estimates sufficiently to use them in projections. The first is consistency across various techniques used to estimate future immigration levels. In the Miami case study, both the national and local experts in the Delphi portion of the study agreed that, on average, 400,000 documented and undocumented immigrants would arrive to live in Dade County (and 150,000 specifically in the City of Miami) over the next decade. This total is close to the average of statistical forecast estimates based on past trends. Best guess projections for the decade, based on analysis of archival data, ranged from 266,700 (using census-derived estimates for estimating undocumented immigration) to 656,400 (using school-based data). Thus, municipal planning based on the minimal, 150,000 figure appears prudent.

The second factor is the congruence of impact-lagged effects with hypothesized expectations. The pattern of changes found in response to immigration in virtually all revenue and expenditure categories corresponded well with theoretical propositions. The predictions of immediate effects on personnel expenditures and direct services such as police, delayed effects on capital expenditures, shifts of expenditures away from general government, and the delayed effects on most revenue sources were all confirmed in the analysis. This confirmation increases confidence in the validity of the estimated-impact models.

PROJECTED IMPACT FOR THE CASE STUDY CITY

The best guess statistical projections for overall immigration to the City of Miami over the next decade ranges from 50,000 to 235,000 documented and undocumented immigrants. The archival impact analysis for the City of Miami indicates each of these immigrants would be expected to cost about $1,391 (1989 dollars) in deflated expenditures for municipal services, and add about $1,118 in deflated general municipal revenue. For 150,000 immigrants, this is a total of nearly $209 million in expenditures and $168 million in revenue within eight years of entry (see Tables 7.1 and 7.2), a total deficit of $41 million.

The 1988 surge in immigration resulted in an estimated 18,525 immigrants arriving in the City of Miami. The delayed effects evidenced in the impact analysis demonstrate that this one-year surge will continue to affect municipal expenditures and revenues for many years in the future. The impact model suggests that the 18,525 immigrants will add more then $25 million to municipal expenditures and $20 million to municipal revenues within nine years of entry.

Breaking down revenue projections by revenue source demonstrates the importance of including intergovernment revenue in the net revenue increase associated with immigration. The impact models demonstrate that the 18,525 immigrants arriving during 1988 and the projected 150,000 immigrants

Table 7.1
Projected Impact of Immigration on Municipal Revenues (Deflated): Net Effect over Nine Years Following Arrival

		Number of Immigrants		
Revenues	1	50,000	150,000	400,000
General Revenue	$920 (4)[a]	$46.0 M[b]	$138.0 M	$368.0 M
Property Tax	−214 (0)	−$10.7 M	−$32.1 M	−$85.6 M
Sales Tax	89 (0)	$4.5 M	$13.4 M	$35.6 M
User Charges	−$245 (0)	−$12.3 M	−$36.8 M	−$98.0 M
Intergovernmental Revenue Total	$1087 (3)	$54.4 M	$163.1 M	$434.8 M
State	$704 (2)	$35.2 M	$105.6 M	$281.6 M
Federal	$417 (4)	$20.9 M	$62.6 M	$166.8 M

[a]Number in parentheses indicates number of years after entry required for occurrence of predominant net effect. For example, the net effect of an immigrant on general revenue becomes positive four years after entry.
[b]M stands for million.

Table 7.2
Projected Impact of Immigration on Municipal Expenditures (Deflated): Net Effect over Nine Years Following Arrival

Expenditures	1	Number of Immigrants		
		50,000	150,000	400,000
General	$1145 (3)[a]	$57.3 M[b]	$171.8 M	$458.0 M
Personnel Services	$802 (0)	$40.1 M	$120.3 M	$320.8 M
Capital	$617 (3)	$30.9 M	$92.6 M	$246.8 M
Police	$304 (0)	$15.2 M	$45.6 M	$121.6 M
Sanitation	$90 (0)	$4.5 M	$13.5 M	$36.0 M
Streets	$222 (4)	$11.1 M	$33.3 M	$88.8 M
Fire	$98 (4)	$4.9 M	$14.7 M	$39.2 M
Sewers	$121 (5)	$6.1 M	$18.2 M	$48.4 M
Parks	$300 (0)	$15.0 M	$45.0 M	$120.0 M
General Government	-$97 (0)	-$4.9 M	-$14.6 M	-$38.8 M
Financial	-$104 (0)	-$5.2 M	-$15.6 M	-$41.6 M
Buildings	$22 (5)	$1.1 M	$3.3 M	$8.8 M
Control	-$2 (0)	-$0.1 M	-$0.3 M	-$0.8 M

[a]Number in parentheses indicates number of years after entry required for occurrence of predominant net effect. For example, the net effect of an immigrant on general expenditures becomes positive three years after entry.
[b]M stands for million.

over the next decade will actually result in a reduction of property tax revenue of about $5 million from the 1988 surge alone, and $39 million over the decade. In addition, user charges will reduce by about $6 million and $45 million, respectively (Table 7.1). On the other hand, net revenue from sales taxes is estimated to increase by about $2 million due to 1988 immigration, and by about $16 million due to the addition of 150,000 more immigrants over the decade. Revenue from intergovernment sources, particularly from the state, is expected to increase by nearly $25 million in response to the 1988 immigration, and by $198 million in response to the arrival of 150,000 more immigrants over the decade.

The importance of the intergovernment category (including federal and state assistance programs for immigrants) in the revenue projections should be underscored. When intergovernment categories are excluded, immigration is associated with a net decrease in revenue. The recent strain in federal and, particularly, state expenditures may severely cut intergovernment transfers to municipalities. If so, net gains predicted based on past trends may fail to materialize. Thus, federal and state policies are crucial in determining the ultimate fiscal impact of immigration on municipal operations.

Expenditure projections can also be broken down by service categories, using the combination of forecast and impact estimates (see Table 7.2). The increase in personnel expenditures exceeds the increase in capital expenditures, but both are substantial. The estimated 18,525 immigrants arriving in 1988 are expected to add more then $18 million to personnel expenditures and nearly $14 million to capital expenditures, while the 150,000 immigrants expected over the next decade are projected to add more then $146 million in personnel expenditures and $112 million in capital expenditures.[1]

In terms of specific services, the largest expenditure increases are expected for parks, police, and streets. The 18,525 immigrants in 1988 are expected to add nearly $7 million to both police and parks expenditures, and $5 million to streets expenditures within nine years of entry. The 150,000 immigrants over the next decade are expected to add more then $55 million to police expenditures, nearly $45 million to parks, and $33 million to expenditures for streets. However, the impact model suggests that general government expenditures will decline in response to immigrant flows. The 18,525 immigrants in 1988 will be associated with a $2 million decline in general government expenditures according to the model, and the 150,000 immigrants anticipated over the next decade will decrease general government expenditures by $14.6 million. All of these predictions are, of course, contingent on the accuracy of the immigration estimates and projections and on the future applicability of the impact model.

The impact of immigration on future revenues and expenditures can also be examined on a yearly basis (see Tables 7.3 through 7.6). Since immigration in a given year is associated with revenue and expenditure changes over the next several years, the overall immigration-induced change in expenditures or revenues in a given year is a function of the immigration level for several years prior to the change. Revenue and expenditure changes in 1990, for example, are a function of immigration in 1990 and in the preceding eight years in the model.

Tables 7.3 through 7.6 indicate projected yearly changes in City of Miami revenues and expenditures based on immigration estimates and projections for eight years following arrival. The revenue projection based on immigration estimates, generated with the ARIMA forecast model, suggests successively larger immigration-induced increases in general revenue, from $10 million in 1990 to $23 million in 1996 (Table 7.3). The rise is a function of increasing intergovernment revenue, particularly revenue from state sources. The projections based on exponential-smoothing estimates of immigration indicate successively larger increases from 1990 ($13.5 million) through 1993 ($18.3 million), and then stable increases (of between $17 and

Table 7.3
**Projected Change in City of Miami Revenues Attributable to Immigration:
ARIMA (Millions of 1989 Dollars)**

Revenue	Year						
	90	91	92	93	94	95	96
General	10.0	12.2	15.5	18.9	20.9	21.7	23.4
Property Tax	-5.2	-5.5	-5.6	-5.6	-5.5	-5.3	-5.5
Sales Tax	2.0	1.9	1.8	1.8	1.9	2.1	2.3
User Charges	-4.4	-4.7	-5.1	-5.4	-5.6	-5.9	-6.2
Intergovernmental Revenue							
Total	15.4	18.1	21.0	23.8	26.7	28.7	28.2
State	10.7	12.7	14.5	16.3	18.0	19.1	18.4
Federal	5.0	5.6	6.6	7.8	9.0	10.1	10.6

Note: Immigration projections used in calculating effects are based on the ARIMA
estimation model for total immigration, using the school-based estimate of undocumented immigration.

Table 7.4
**Projected Change in City of Miami Revenues Attributable to Immigration:
Smoothing (Millions of 1989 Dollars)**

Revenue	Year						
	90	91	92	93	94	95	96
General	13.5	15.7	17.4	18.3	17.8	17.0	17.6
Property Tax	-4.3	-4.0	-3.6	-3.4	-3.1	-3.0	-3.2
Sales Tax	1.4	1.2	1.2	1.3	1.4	1.6	1.4
User Charges	-4.1	-4.0	-4.1	-4.2	-4.2	-4.1	-4.2
Intergovernmental Revenue							
Total	16.6	19.1	20.7	21.5	21.8	21.0	18.6
State	11.0	12.5	13.5	13.7	13.6	12.8	10.9
Federal	5.6	6.4	7.2	7.8	8.2	8.2	7.7

Note: Immigration projections used in calculating effects are based on the exponential-smoothing estimation model for total immigration, using the school-based estimate of undocumented immigration.

Table 7.5
Projected Change in City of Miami Expenditures Attributable to Immigration: ARIMA (Millions of 1989 Dollars)

Service	Year						
	90	91	92	93	94	95	96
General	16.1	17.7	20.2	22.9	25.4	27.7	29.2
Personnel	14.6	16.0	17.4	18.6	19.5	20.2	20.7
Capital	8.2	8.7	9.9	11.3	12.7	14.1	15.5
Police	5.4	6.1	6.7	7.2	7.6	7.9	7.9
Sanitation	1.4	1.5	1.7	1.9	2.0	2.2	2.3
Streets	2.9	3.1	3.6	4.1	4.7	5.2	5.6
Fire	1.0	1.1	1.4	1.7	1.8	1.8	2.4
Sewer	2.0	1.7	1.8	1.9	1.9	2.1	2.9
Parks	6.4	6.6	6.3	6.1	7.5	9.4	7.9
General Gov't.	-2.0	-2.1	-2.2	-2.2	-2.3	-2.3	-2.4
Financial Admin.	-2.2	-2.3	-2.3	-2.4	-2.5	-2.7	-2.7
Public Buildings	0.3	0.3	0.3	0.4	0.5	0.5	0.6

Note: Immigration projections used in calculating effects are based on the ARIMA estimation model for total immigration, using the school-based estimate of undocumented immigration.

$18 million yearly) through 1996 (see Table 7.4). Again, the increases are primarily a function of changes in revenue from intergovernment sources.

Virtually all expenditure categories show steadily larger increases between 1990 and 1996 when the ARIMA model is used to estimate immigration (see Table 7.5). General government expenditures associated with immigration grow from $16.1 million in 1990 to $29.2 million in 1996, including steady increases in both personnel and capital expenditures. Projected expenditures associated with immigration are more stable when calculated using immigration estimates based on exponential-smoothing models (see Table 7.6). General expenditures rise from $16.6 million in 1990 to $21.5 million in 1994 and then fall slightly by 1996, when general expenditures are predicted to have an immigration-induced increase of $20.4 million.

The increases in expenditures are consistently larger than the increases in revenue. The gap between expenditure and revenue increases begins at about $6 million in 1990, narrows to about $4 million in 1993, and returns to

Table 7.6
Projected Change in City of Miami Expenditures Attributable to Immigration: Smoothing (Millions of 1989 Dollars)

Service	Year						
	90	91	92	93	94	95	96
General	16.6	18.1	19.7	20.9	21.5	21.4	20.4
Personnel	13.5	13.9	14.2	14.2	14.0	13.5	13.0
Capital	8.6	9.1	10.1	11.0	11.5	11.7	11.7
Police	5.1	5.4	5.6	5.6	5.4	5.2	4.8
Sanitation	1.4	1.5	1.5	1.6	1.6	1.6	1.6
Streets	3.1	3.3	3.7	4.0	4.2	4.2	4.1
Fire	1.4	1.5	1.6	1.7	1.7	1.7	2.3
Sewer	1.7	1.5	1.5	1.7	1.9	2.1	2.6
Parks	3.8	4.1	4.5	4.9	5.9	6.3	2.9
General Gov't.	-1.7	-1.6	-1.6	-1.6	-1.5	-1.5	-1.6
Financial Admin.	-1.7	-1.7	-1.7	-1.7	-1.8	-1.8	-1.5
Public Buildings	0.3	0.3	0.4	0.4	0.4	0.4	0.4

Note: Immigration projections used in calculating effects are based on the exponential-smoothing estimation model for total immigration, using the school-based estimate of undocumented immigration.

about $6 million by 1996 when ARIMA-based projections are compared. The gap fluctuates between $2 and $4 million when exponential-smoothing projections are compared. The gap will become much larger if intergovernment response to immigration declines or is delayed for an extended period of time.

For many services and revenue sources, the increases or decreases are relatively stable. In part, this reflects the tendency of forecasted immigration values to move toward average values, similar to a regression to the mean effect. The statistical forecasts are unable to predict sudden shifts in immigration, such as the Mariel influx in 1980, the Central American influx of the late 1980s, or the recent wave of Haitian and Cuban refugees. But the stabilization of revenue and expenditure changes is also a function of the multiyear impact of immigration on revenues and expenditures. The lagged impact of immigration spreads the effect of immigration's peaks and valleys over a period of years. Short-run targeted assistance is useful in dealing with the immediate needs of an influx of immigrants, but does not deal with long-term changes in expenditures and revenues.

INTERPRETING THE MODEL

Projections assume that past association between immigration and municipal revenues and expenditures will continue in the future. As discussed earlier, this is not an easy assumption to make. The recent fiscal problems at the federal and state level are likely to have a major impact on real, as opposed to projected, revenues and expenditures during the next decade. For example, the State of Florida is experiencing serious revenue problems as a result of the recent economic downturn, and has sued the federal government in an attempt to retrieve immigration-based expenditures. In addition, recent immigrant arrivals may not translate into increased revenue, especially increased state revenue, as readily as they have in the past. Immigrants will have a more difficult time establishing themselves economically. Their effect on the community's economic health and on revenues related to economic health, including some state funding formulas, will be minimized. This dampening effect may be worsened if the likelihood of special targeted state or federal assistance drops in periods of local fiscal stress.

Since municipal expenditures depend in large part on revenue projections, immigrants' effects on expenditures can also be expected to be reduced. The demand for public services will continue to increase, but municipalities will simply not have the financial resources to accommodate the additional demand. In fact, the demand for some services (social services, police services, and parks) is likely to be higher because of the adverse effects of the economic downturn on the immigrants. The likely impact of decreased aid will be a decrease in per capita expenditures on the local level as immigrants add to the population being served but not to parallel revenue increases.

Further, if the trends continue there may be an associated decline in service quality and citizen satisfaction, and increased pressure on local government employees and elected officials to produce more with less. Since government cannot address the demand, we are likely to see an increase in nongovernment service provision and efforts to shift high-cost groups out of the community. As a result, the community may become less charitable about receiving new immigrants and may see an increase in the flight of wealthier residents out of the area. A potential danger on the municipal level is the evolution of transitional immigration enclaves into permanent multigenerational ghettos.

CONCLUSION

This book focused on the impact of immigration on municipal expenditures and revenues. As discussed earlier, a change in expenditures captures only a part of the overall social, political, and economic impact. Changes in workload, service quality, working conditions, workforce morale, and so on may occur with no change in expenditures. Overall, expenditure levels are constrained by revenues, limiting major adjustments in response to immigration. The impact is then transferred to these other categories, and the effects become less documented and more difficult to measure. A part of the research agenda for the future is the documentation of these effects.

The model presented in this book provides local government administrators a mechanism for examining immigration's impacts on their jurisdiction's financial position. The model provides a relatively low-cost technique that is more accurate than estimates and forecasts from other sources because of its sensitivity to local factors and history. The process involved in developing this model included the following steps:

- An examination of historical data to determine the level of immigration in the past and analyze the demographic characteristics of past immigrants
- A survey of recent immigrants examining their characteristics which impact government services, their reasons for immigrating, and the potential impact of government on immigrants' decisions, as well as their future plans
- A multiphase survey (Delphi) of local and national experts to determine their assessment of past and future impacts and their forecast of future immigration levels
- The development of a set of models capturing the impact of past immigration on municipal revenues and service expenditures
- The development of statistical projections of future immigration trends
- The combination of immigration projections with past impact models to forecast the impact of immigration on municipal revenues and service expenditures over the next decade

One of the lessons cutting across the findings from the components of the study is the complexity and difficulty of an assessment of immigration impact on municipal services. Immigration and immigrants are not monolithic. The effects of a particular immigrant varies, depending on various characteristics, such as nationality, language, socioeconomic status, INS status, race, cultural norms, family characteristics, and the length of time in the United States and in the local community.

As noted, these factors affect the level of services needed by the immigrant, the services demanded by the immigrant, the willingness of the immigrant to utilize services, the eligibility of the immigrant for services, and the difficulty of assessing and responding to additional service demands. These factors also affect the immigrant's ability to successfully become a part of the community, and the level of contribution made by the immigrant to the community's resources and economic health. Last, immigrant characteristics affect future immigration levels, as well as the drawing power of the immigrant on potential future immigrants.

The impact of individual characteristics is further conditioned by the characteristics of the community that they have entered, particularly existing community support networks (most notably immigrant enclaves), the community's experience with immigration, and prevailing attitudes toward immigrants. Immigrant enclaves provide matching immigrants alternative social supports and increased access to government services. They can reduce the immediate impact of language, cultural norms, INS status, and other disadvantageous characteristics for the arriving immigrant.

Just as the immigrant side of the effects equation is complex and multifaceted, the government effects side is equally complex. Immigration impact varies across levels of government, across government jurisdictions at the same level, across services within government jurisdictions, and across revenue and expenditure categories. Local government is impacted particularly heavily, because they are direct service providers and most frequently in contact with immigrants. The profusion of cultural differences accompanying immigration has also created problems in communication and government service provision that cut across service areas, with greatest impacts on police services, emergency medical services, education, and solid waste disposal.

Within the municipalities, some services are affected more then others. Both the Delphi and impact analysis suggest that basic municipal services, particularly those involving direct resident contact (such as police, sanitation, and parks), are strongly affected. The field-survey analysis demonstrates that the impact grows over time as immigrants become aware of services and increase reliance on government. This analysis also confirmed that the impact of the typical immigrant on expenditures in most categories grows over time. The expenditure increase comes early for police, sanitation, and parks. These services all show a net increase from the year of entry forward. Other services, such as streets, fire, sewers, and capital expenditures, generally have an initial decline in response to immigration and only show a net increase four or five years after entry.

Municipal funding, constrained by relatively fixed revenues, is apparently shifted to high-impact services at the expense of services with less substantial short-term needs. General government expenditures, according to the model, actually have a net decrease in response to immigration over the entire study period, suggesting that resources are siphoned off to pay direct-service costs. But immigration does not reduce general government or low-impact service needs. The costs are internalized through increased workloads or show up as changes in service quality, which are harder to measure.

Immigration also impacts revenue sources in different ways. According to the models, some of the traditionally important revenue sources, such as property taxes, actually suffered a net loss in response to immigration for the first nine years after entry. Other sources, notably intergovernment revenues and user-based charges, are much more sensitive to immigration.

The burden for providing services to immigrants, however, is not shared equally. Within high-immigrant localities, some jurisdictions receive more immigrants than others. This study suggests that these municipalities serve as a sort of training ground for immigrants. Most of the Delphi experts perceived that immigration places short-term burdens on government, but in the long run immigration is beneficial to the community. Unfortunately, it appears that long-term benefits do not accrue to the jurisdictions bearing the original costs. The archival data show that a disproportionate number of arriving immigrants reside in certain municipalities. As these immigrants become established economically and socially, they move to other, more prosperous jurisdictions and are replaced by a new set of arriving immigrants. Therefore, the jurisdictions with a disproportionate share of new immigrants bear the initial socialization and conditioning costs without the benefit of subsequent increasing revenues and community development.

The options of government, particularly at the municipal level, for managing and anticipating immigration impact are limited. The reasons for immigration to the United States, primarily political, economic, or family reunification, are virtually immune to municipal manipulation. The field survey indicates that channels of information available to government, such as television, radio, newspapers, and embassies, play a very limited role in the immigrant's decision to come to the United States. Most immigrants decided to migrate based on information from family and friends in their home country; in essence, their personal social networks.

Moreover, once in the United States, the choice of residency depends much more on the location of fellow countrymen and family than on any municipal policy intervention. The archival data confirm this: Well over 90 percent of the documented immigrants arriving in Miami have family in the area. The archival data also indicate the futility of resettlement programs. Virtually all of the Mariel and Haitian immigrants of 1980, many of whom were initially resettled to other parts of the United States, resided in Miami by the time they were given immigrant status in 1987 and 1988.

Not only is it difficult for government to manage the flow of immigrants, it is virtually impossible to monitor the number of immigrants that do reside in a particular community for any length of time. The data on legal immigrants are outdated by the time they are available to municipalities. Estimates of the undocumented population are only available for census years, and even then represent at least a 50 to 75 percent undercount. To compound these problems, there is no reliable information on the movement of immigrants between American cities after immigration, or the level of out-migration when immigrants return to their home country. This makes it very difficult to address the needs of immigrants and to anticipate future immigration.

Statistical forecasts based on current immigration data are of short-term utility. The most important kind of influx to anticipate is the large-scale shift, which also is the most difficult kind of immigration event to predict. The various techniques illustrated in this book show promise as aids in predicting immigration and immigration impacts, but they are not without limitations. Since the statistical forecasts and impact models have large margins of error, the necessity of sound, insightful local knowledge to cope with this uncertainty is necessitated. Delphi forecasts can be more precise but, as suggested in the Miami case, experts are reluctant to provide specific estimates of something with as much uncertainty as future immigration levels.

The techniques detailed in this work provide the municipal administrator with the ability to begin documenting and analyzing local immigration impacts. By emphasizing the importance of local context and insights, the impact model addresses two specific needs of municipal decision makers. First, the information produced permits the development of proactive municipal policy, allowing decision makers to be less at the mercy of immigration fluctuations. Second, the model enables municipalities to concretely demonstrate the impacts of immigration, supporting their requests for reimbursement and additonal funding from county, state, and federal levels of government.

NOTE

1. Note that impact was only examined for nine years after entry. Any effect on expenditures or revenue after nine years has not been captured in the analysis.

Field Survey Instrument

IMMIGRANT FIELD SURVEY
English Version

     Hello, my name is _____ and I work for Florida International University. The University is conducting a study in order to better understand the special needs and problems of new people coming into the south Florida area. We are collecting information by asking a number of new arrivals about their plans and their decision to come to south Florida. We also are interested in your opinions on a number of matters. The answers you give will be combined with the answers of hundreds of other people and used to determine what are the most common needs and problems of new immigrants. None of this information will be given to INS or any other government agency or private organization. Your individual answers will be kept confidential and you do not have to give your name if you do not want to. You do not have to answer any questions that you do not want to either. The interview should take about 30 to 45 minutes.

INTERVIEW NUMBER:
INTERVIEW SITE:
INTERVIEWER:
DATE OF INTERVIEW:
REFERRAL SOURCE:

DATE OF ARRIVAL IN U.S.:
DATE OF ARRIVAL IN S. FLA.:
DATE OF BIRTH:

Section I. In this first section I would like to ask you some questions about how you decided to come to the United States.

1. What was the single most important reason you decided to come to the United States?

Any additional reasons? *Interviewer - Please List*

2. Could you tell me some of the information that helped you the most to decide to immigrate?

Can you remember where you first heard this information?

3. Did you make any special preparations or plans for your life in the United States prior to immigrating? *[Interviewer - Circle letter if mentioned.]*

a. saved money (Amount_____)
b. saved clothes or other household goods
c. learned English
d. learned a new job skill
e. contacted relatives here
f. contacted friends here
g. contacted potential employers
h. none
i. others *(Please List)*

How long before your actual immigration did you begin to make the preparations?

4. Did you have a job waiting for you?   Yes   No
    If yes, who made the arrangements for you to have a job waiting for you?

5. Who did you come to the United States with?

a. alone
b. with family *[Interviewer: Please List Number, Ages and Relationships]*
c. with friends
d. other co-workers
e. other neighborhood people from prior country
f. other unknown countrymen

6. Did you watch U.S. television or listen to U.S. radio while in your prior country? *If yes, please circle all relevant categories*

a. TV News Shows
b. TV Entertainment Shows
c. Radio News
d. Radio Entertainment/Music

7. How many times prior to immigrating to the United States did you visit? _____

8. I'm going to read you a list of people or places where you could have gotten information which helped you decide to immigrate. Please tell me approximately how much information you got from each source that helped you decide to immigrate. You will use this same scale in some later questions.
[Interviewer - Hand Likert scale and explain use.]

(A)ALL	(M)MOST	(S)SOME	(L)JUST A LITTLE		(N)NONE		(NS)NOT SURE	
	a. family in U.S.		A	M	S	L	N	NS
	b. friends in U.S.		A	M	S	L	N	NS
	c. family in Prior		A	M	S	L	N	NS
	d. friends in Prior		A	M	S	L	N	NS
	e. U.S. Government		A	M	S	L	N	NS
	f. Prior Government		A	M	S	L	N	NS
	g. newspapers (U.S.)		A	M	S	L	N	NS
	h. radio (U.S.)		A	M	S	L	N	NS
	i. television (U.S.)		A	M	S	L	N	NS
	j. newspapers (Prior)		A	M	S	L	N	NS
	k. radio (Prior)		A	M	S	L	N	NS
	l. television (Prior)		A	M	S	L	N	NS
	m. yourself from prior visits		A	M	S	L	N	NS
	n. church		A	M	S	L	N	NS
	o. other *(Please List)*		A	M	S	L	N	NS

Now I'd like to ask you some questions about how you decided where to live in the United States.

1. Did you decide where to live before or after your arrival here?   Before _____ After _____

2. Were there people (family/friends) waiting for you when you arrived? Yes___ No___
     Did you stay with them? Yes___ No___
     Are you still living with them? Yes___ No___

3. If you did not stay with waiting family or friends when you first arrived, where did you live?

4. Where do you now live? *[Interviewer- If just arriving immigrant - Where do you plan to live?]*

5. Did you find your own place to live: *[Interviewer - Ask as appropriate]*

                    when you first arrived.   Yes___ No___
                    most recently.   Yes___ No___

          If no, who found you housing?

6. Do you currently live:
      a. alone
      b. with family
      c. with friends
      d. in a boarding house
      e. other

7. When you first came to this country what influenced your decision about where to live? *[Interviewer - Give the person the card with the list of choices. Circle items cited, list others.]*

      a. cost
      b. availability
      c. first place offered

d. closeness to work
e. closeness to relatives
f. wanted to live in this neighborhood
g. other [ethnic group] already living here
h. mother language spoken here
i. housing arranged by others
j. other

8. I'm going to read you the same list of people or places we used earlier. How much information did you get from each of the following about where to live in the United States?

(A)ALL   (M)MOST   (S)SOME   (L)JUST A LITTLE   (N)NONE   (NS)NOT SURE

a. family in U.S.	A	M	S	L	N	NS
b. friends in U.S.	A	M	S	L	N	NS
c. family in Prior	A	M	S	L	N	NS
d. friends in Prior	A	M	S	L	N	NS
e. U.S. Government	A	M	S	L	N	NS
f. Prior Government	A	M	S	L	N	NS
g. newspapers (U.S.)	A	M	S	L	N	NS
h. radio (U.S.)	A	M	S	L	N	NS
I. television (U.S.)	A	M	S	L	N	NS
j. newspapers (Prior)	A	M	S	L	N	NS
k. radio (Prior)	A	M	S	L	N	NS
l. television (Prior)	A	M	S	L	N	NS
m. yourself from prior visits	A	M	S	L	N	NS
n. church	A	M	S	L	N	NS
o. other *(Please List)*	A	M	S	L	N	NS

Section II. In this section I'd like to ask you about what you expected life to be like in the United States and what life was like for you in the country you came from.

1. When you were thinking of coming to the United States, what did you think it would be like? *[Interviewer - Do not read list, but circle letter if an item is mentioned. When a particular condition is mentioned, probe if expectations were that conditions would be better, worse, or the same as conditions in prior country.]*

a. living conditions	Better	Worse	Same
b. job opportunities	Better	Worse	Same
c. wages	Better	Worse	Same
d. local government services	Better	Worse	Same
e. police protection	Better	Worse	Same
f. material goods	Better	Worse	Same
g. political freedom	Better	Worse	Same
h. health or medical care	Better	Worse	Same
i. education	Better	Worse	Same
j. children's opportunities	Better	Worse	Same
k. crime	Better	Worse	Same
l. food	Better	Worse	Same
m. amenities	Better	Worse	Same
n. personal safety	Better	Worse	Same
o. others *(Please List)*	Better	Worse	Same

2. In the country you came from who did you live with? *[Interviewer - probe if extended family.]*

3. In the country you came from how often did you travel?

      Abroad _____
      Within the country _____
      Were you able to travel freely?   Yes___ No___

4. Are there children or immediate family members still living in the country you came from?

5. What was your occupation in the country you came from?

6. Some people are quite active in politics and in their communities, while others prefer not to take an active part. During the last four years before moving to the U.S. did you:

a. vote in an election	YES	NO
b. work for a political party	YES	NO
c. donate money to the poor	YES	NO
d. spend a day helping out a neighbor or a friend	YES	NO
e. be an active member in a church group	YES	NO
f. go to a political meeting	YES	NO

7. Once more using the same scale and list. Before you came here how important was each of the following as a source of information about what life would be like in the United States?

(A)ALL   (M)MOST   (S)SOME   (L)JUST A LITTLE   (N)NONE   (NS)NOT SURE

	A	M	S	L	N	NS
a. family in U.S.	A	M	S	L	N	NS
b. friends in U.S.	A	M	S	L	N	NS
c. family in Prior	A	M	S	L	N	NS
d. friends in Prior	A	M	S	L	N	NS
e. U.S. Government	A	M	S	L	N	NS
f. Prior Government	A	M	S	L	N	NS
g. newspapers (U.S.)	A	M	S	L	N	NS
h. radio (U.S.)	A	M	S	L	N	NS
i. television (U.S.)	A	M	S	L	N	NS
j. newspapers (Prior)	A	M	S	L	N	NS
k. radio (Prior)	A	M	S	L	N	NS
l. television (Prior)	A	M	S	L	N	NS
m. yourself from prior visits	A	M	S	L	N	NS
n. church	A	M	S	L	N	NS
o. other *(Please List)*	A	M	S	L	N	NS

Section III. These next questions ask about how you solve problems and your plans for the future.

1. In the United States what person or persons would you go to for help if you had the following problems?
[Interviewer - Give the person the card which lists choices. Do not read list.]

	U.S.	Prior Country
a. if you were ill	——	——
b. if you needed a place to live	——	——
c. if you had something stolen from you	——	——
d. if you were having arguments with your neighbor	——	——
e. if you needed a job	——	——
f. if you had a question about a law	——	——
g. if you had a question about your rights in America	——	——
h. if you felt you were not being treated fairly by someone	——	——
i. if you didn't have food to eat	——	——
j. if you had a fire	——	——
k. if you needed a ride to the doctor or hospital	——	——
l. if you were assaulted	——	——
m. if you didn't have running water	——	——
n. if you needed your trash or garbage taken away	——	——

[Interviewer - Code from following list of choices:]

1. no one, handle it myself
2. family member
3. friend
4. church, priest, or clergyman
5. neighborhood person
6. boss
7. co-worker
8. local doctor
9. landlord
10. lawyer
11. policeman
12. city official
13. not sure, don't know
14. other (Please List)
15. newspapers/media

2. Who would you have contacted in the country you came from if you had the same problems?
[Interviewer - Ask the person to choose from the same list]

3. Since your arrival in the U.S., have you been referred for social services by any government agency, church, or private organization?
[Interviewer - If yes - list referral sources and services provided]

4. Have you ever personally, gone to see, spoken to, or written to some member of local government about some needs or problem?

Prior Country	Yes____	No____
In the U.S.	Yes____	No____

[If yes]
    Was the issue primarily of concern just to you, your friends and family, or was it an issue of wider social or neighborhood concern?

4. If you were interested in working for the government, what do you think would be the best way to get a government job?

Now I'd like to ask you about your future plans.

1. Within the next 5 years do you plan to:
        (Interviewer - read choices)

        a. bring additional family to the United States
        b. go to school
        c. learn a new job skill or trade
        d. change jobs
        e. become a U.S. citizen
        f. learn English
        g. move (where _____)
        (Choose answer from list below)

                [Interviewer - Enter appropriate category for (g)].
                1) to a different place within same city
                2) to a different city with same county
                3) to a different part of Florida
                4) to a different part of the United States
                5) to a different country
                6) return to original country

We're nearing the end, thank you for your patience.

Section V. In the following section I will read a number of sentences and I will ask you if you strongly agree, somewhat agree, are neutral about, somewhat disagree, or strongly disagree with each statement. For example, if I say "the weather in the United States is good" and you feel the weather in America is hardly ever good then you would strongly disagree with that sentence, if you feel that the weather is good most of the time you would somewhat agree, and if you felt it was good and bad about equally you would be neutral. The card I am giving you lists the choices. Do you understand how this section works? *[Interviewer - Confirm Understanding]*

(ST) Strongly Agree	(N) Neutral	(SD) Somewhat Disagree
(SA) Somewhat Agree		(STD) Strongly Disagree

1. I feel safe walking alone at night in the neighborhood I now live in.   ST SA N SD STD

2. It is difficult to find work in the United States.   ST SA N SD STD

3. Television news in the U.S. is accurate most of time.   ST SA N SD STD

4. In the U.S. the police are often justified where they use violence. ST SA N SD STD

5. Most of what is printed in U.S. newspapers is accurate. ST SA N SD STD

6. In the U.S., most crimes are solved. ST SA N SD STD

7. Television shows about crime in the U.S. are realistic? ST SA N SD STD

8. Most criminals when caught should be sent to prison. ST SA N SD STD

9. The news I hear on the radio is mostly accurate. ST SA N SD STD

10. The crime problem where I now live is not very serious. ST SA N SD STD

11. In the U.S. the police are effective in fighting crime. ST SA N SD STD

12. People who make more money should pay a larger percentage
of their earnings in taxes. ST SA N SD STD

13. Marriage between people of different religions is wrong. ST SA N SD STD

14. It is easy to earn money in the United States? ST SA N SD STD

15. Society should try to rehabilitate criminals. ST SA N SD STD

16. More police are needed in the U.S. ST SA N SD STD

17. Marriage between people of different races is wrong. ST SA N SD STD

18. More courts are needed in the US. ST SA N SD STD

19. More bus service is needed in the U.S. ST SA N SD STD

20. Better garbage collection is needed in the U.S. ST SA N SD STD

21. More prisons are needed in the U.S. ST SA N SD STD

22. Better medical care is needed in the U.S. ST SA N SD STD

23. More programs for youth are needed in the U.S. ST SA N SD STD

24. More parks are needed in the U.S. ST SA N SD STD

25. More programs for the elderly are needed in the U.S. ST SA N SD STD

**Now I would like to read you some statements that concern government in general. Don't respond
to the statements with any particular government in mind. We'll use the same card.**

26. Much of the time you can trust government
officials to do what is right. ST SA N SD STD

27. Government officials consider the opinions and concerns
of people like yourself when making decisions. ST SA N SD STD

28. If you had some complaint about a local government action and
took your complaint to the government offices, the official would
pay a lot of attention to what you say. ST SA N SD STD

29. Most government officials are not really interested
in the problems of average people.   ST SA N SD STD

30. Government is pretty much run by a few big interests looking
out for themselves.   ST SA N SD STD

31. People in government usually waste a lot of
the money collected as taxes.   ST SA N SD STD

32. Quite a few of the people running governments
are smart people who usually know what they are doing.   ST SA N SD STD

33. The best way to get a government official to do
something give him something for his trouble.   ST SA N SD STD

34. The quickest way to get help from a government office is to
make friends with one of the officials of the office.   ST SA N SD STD

35. The people running government are crooked.   ST SA N SD STD

36. It is the responsibility of government to meet everyone's needs,
even if a person is sick, poor, unemployed, or old.   ST SA N SD STD

37. Government should see to it that every person has a job and a
good standard of living.   ST SA N SD STD

38. Government should just let each person get ahead on his own.   ST SA N SD STD

39. Government is pretty much run for the benefit of all the people. ST SA N SD STD

Section VI. (Demographic Information) Thanks for being patient, this is the last section of our interview and now I'd like to ask you some questions about yourself

1. What is your age: _____

2. Sex: _____

3. How many years of school have you completed? (Yrs.) _____

4. Number of children living with you at home: _____
(List ages and languages)

5. Do you have a television where you now live?   YES ___ NO ___

6. Do you have a favorite and second favorite television show? 1)_____
2)_____

7. On the average about how many hours of television do you watch daily? _____

8. What radio station do you listen to the most? _____

9. What newspaper do you most often read? _____

10. In the U.S., what is your main source of news about your prior country?

11. What is your main source of news about events in the U.S.?

12. Have you or any member of your household been the victim of a crime within the past 12 months?

If yes: in the U.S. or Prior Country? _____

Do you remember what kind of crime it was? *(List)*

13. Do you have any special health needs? *(chronic illnesses, medications, etc.)*

14. What is your profession or trade? _____

15. Do you have special work skills? *(List)*

16. Language: (Mother tongue) _____

A) English:	speak _____	read _____	write _____
B) Spanish:	speak _____	read _____	write _____
C) French:	speak _____	read _____	write _____
D) Creole:	speak _____	read _____	write _____
E) Other:	speak _____	read _____	write _____

17. Religion: _____

18. Country of Birth: _____

19. Race: _____

20. Amount of current savings: _____

21. Weekly family income in U.S.: _____

22. Approximately how much did your immediate family earn weekly in the country you came from? _____

23. Number of family members currently working in the U.S.: _____

Thank you very much for talking with me. Your answers are important and will be very helpful. If you are willing we would like to talk with you in 6 months to a year to see how you are adjusting to life in the United States. Would you be willing to give a second interview?

[If yes: Interviewer - Collect contact information]

What will be the best way to contact you?

Contact Person:	_____
Phone:	_____
Address:	_____

Delphi Survey
(First Round)

LOCAL EXPERTS QUESTIONNAIRE

Name:

I wish to receive a copy of the final report.
   yes _____   no _____

I. Impact of Immigration

1. In your opinion what has been the impact of immigration on your community?

2. In your opinion what has been the impact of immigration on the following municipal services and responsibilities:

1) police:

2) emergency medical:

3) waste disposal:

4) fire:

5) water/sewage:

6) government revenue:

7) general government

8) other:

3. In your opinion what will be the impact of future immigration on municipal services in South Florida?

II. Demographics

Circle numbered responses where appropriate

1. Education:
    1. High School Graduate
    2. Some college
    3 College Graduate
    4. Completed Graduate Degree (MA,PHD,MD,ETC.)

2. Age _____.

3. Racial background:
    1. White   4. Native American
    2. Black   5. other
    3. Asian

4. Would you classify yourself as:
    1. a 1st Generation immigrant
    2. a 2nd Generation immigrant
    3. a 3rd Generation or more immigrant

5. Which of the following languages do you:

	Speak	Read	Write
1. Spanish	a	b	c
2. French	a	b	c
3. Creole	a	b	c
4. Portuguese	a	b	c
5. other			
_____	a	b	c
6. other			
_____	a	b	c

6. Number of years of residence in South Florida: _____.

7. Briefly list work experiences that are particularly important for your current perception and knowledge regarding immigration.

Name of Organization	Year Began	Year Ended	Job Title

NATIONAL EXPERTS QUESTIONNAIRE

Name:

I wish to receive a copy of the final report.
        yes _____   no _____

I. Impact of Immigration

1. From which countries do you expect most immigrants to come between now and the end of the century?

2. Why do you expect the immigrant flows to originate in these specific countries?

3. In your opinion which geographical regions of the United States are likely to receive the immigrants from which countries?

U.S. Region	Countries	U.S. Region	Countries
1) New England		6) East South Central	
2) Middle Atlantic		7) West South Central	
3) East North Central		8) Mountain	
4) West North Central		9) North Pacific Coast	
5) South Atlantic		10) South Pacific Coast	

5. Why do you expect the immigrants to settle in these specific regions?

II. Demographics

Circle numbered responses where appropriate

1. Education:
   1. High School Graduate
   2. Some college
   3 College Graduate
   4. Completed Graduate Degree (MA,PHD,MD,ETC.)

2. Age _____.

3. Racial background:
   1. White   4. Native American
   2. Black   5. other
   3. Asian

4. Would you classify yourself as:
   1. a 1st Generation immigrant
   2. a 2nd Generation immigrant
   3. a 3rd Generation or more immigrant

5. Which of the following languages do you:

	Speak	Read	Write
1. Spanish	a	b	c
2. French	a	b	c
3. Creole	a	b	c
4. Portuguese	a	b	c
5. other			
_____	a	b	c
6. other			
_____	a	b	c

6. Briefly list work experiences that are particularly important for your current perception and knowledge regarding immigration.

Name of Organization	Year Began	Year Ended	Job Title

Delphi Survey (Second Round)

LOCAL EXPERTS QUESTIONNAIRE

Please circle the percentage range appropriate for each country of origin.

1. What percentage of immigrants settling in Dade County will be undocumented?

Cuba	0-25%	26-50%	51-75%	76-100%
Haiti	0-25%	26-50%	51-75%	76-100%
Nicaragua	0-25%	26-50%	51-75%	76-100%
Guatemala	0-25%	26-50%	51-75%	76-100%
El Salvador	0-25%	26-50%	51-75%	76-100%
Honduras	0-25%	26-50%	51-75%	76-100%
Other:				
_____	0-25%	26-50%	51-75%	76-100%
_____	0-25%	26-50%	51-75%	76-100%

2. What percentage of immigrants settling in Dade County will be able to speak English?

Cuba	0-25%	26-50%	51-75%	76-100%
Haiti	0-25%	26-50%	51-75%	76-100%
Nicaragua	0-25%	26-50%	51-75%	76-100%
Guatemala	0-25%	26-50%	51-75%	76-100%
El Salvador	0-25%	26-50%	51-75%	76-100%
Honduras	0-25%	26-50%	51-75%	76-100%
Other:				
_____	0-25%	26-50%	51-75%	76-100%
_____	0-25%	26-50%	51-75%	76-100%

3. What percentage of immigrants settling in Dade County will have relatives, friends, or established communities of support upon arrival?

Cuba	0-25%	26-50%	51-75%	76-100%
Haiti	0-25%	26-50%	51-75%	76-100%
Nicaragua	0-25%	26-50%	51-75%	76-100%
Guatemala	0-25%	26-50%	51-75%	76-100%
El Salvador	0-25%	26-50%	51-75%	76-100%
Honduras	0-25%	26-50%	51-75%	76-100%
Other:				
_____	0-25%	26-50%	51-75%	76-100%
_____	0-25%	26-50%	51-75%	76-100%

4. What percentage will have white collar skills?

Cuba	0-25%	26-50%	51-75%	76-100%
Haiti	0-25%	26-50%	51-75%	76-100%
Nicaragua	0-25%	26-50%	51-75%	76-100%
Guatemala	0-25%	26-50%	51-75%	76-100%
El Salvador	0-25%	26-50%	51-75%	76-100%
Honduras	0-25%	26-50%	51-75%	76-100%
Other:				
_____	0-25%	26-50%	51-75%	76-100%
_____	0-25%	26-50%	51-75%	76-100%

5. What percentage will have blue collar skills?

Cuba	0-25%	26-50%	51-75%	76-100%
Haiti	0-25%	26-50%	51-75%	76-100%
Nicaragua	0-25%	26-50%	51-75%	76-100%
Guatemala	0-25%	26-50%	51-75%	76-100%
El Salvador	0-25%	26-50%	51-75%	76-100%
Honduras	0-25%	26-50%	51-75%	76-100%
Other:				
_____	0-25%	26-50%	51-75%	76-100%
_____	0-25%	26-50%	51-75%	76-100%

6. What percentage will have no job skills applicable in the United States?

Cuba	0-25%	26-50%	51-75%	76-100%
Haiti	0-25%	26-50%	51-75%	76-100%
Nicaragua	0-25%	26-50%	51-75%	76-100%
Guatemala	0-25%	26-50%	51-75%	76-100%
El Salvador	0-25%	26-50%	51-75%	76-100%

Honduras	0-25%	26-50%	51-75%	76-100%
Other:				
_____	0-25%	26-50%	51-75%	76-100%
_____	0-25%	26-50%	51-75%	76-100%

7. What percentage of immigrants settling in Dade County, Florida are likely to engage in criminal activity?

Cuba	0-25%	26-50%	51-75%	76-100%
Haiti	0-25%	26-50%	51-75%	76-100%
Nicaragua	0-25%	26-50%	51-75%	76-100%
Guatemala	0-25%	26-50%	51-75%	76-100%
El Salvador	0-25%	26-50%	51-75%	76-100%
Honduras	0-25%	26-50%	51-75%	76-100%
Other:				
_____	0-25%	26-50%	51-75%	76-100%
_____	0-25%	26-50%	51-75%	76-100%

8. Please rank order the impact of incoming immigrants on each service for each of the counties listed below. (7 indicates strongest impact and 1 indicates weakest impact.)

	Police	Fire	EMS	Waste	Water/ Sewer	Gov't Revenue	General Gov't
Cuba	____	____	____	____	____	____	____
Haiti	____	____	____	____	____	____	____
Nicaragua	____	____	____	____	____	____	____
Guatemala	____	____	____	____	____	____	____
El Salvador	____	____	____	____	____	____	____
Honduras	____	____	____	____	____	____	____
Other:							
_____	____	____	____	____	____	____	____
_____	____	____	____	____	____	____	____

9. Please give an estimate for the total number of immigrants, documented and undocumented you believe will settle in Dade County in:

1989 _____

1990 - 2000 _____

10. Estimate the percentages of these immigrants who will be from the following countries:

	1989	1990 - 2000
Cuba	____	____
Haiti	____	____
Nicaragua	____	____

	1989	1990 - 2000
Guatemala	____	____
El Salvador	____	____
Honduras	____	____
Other:		
_____	____	____
_____	____	____

11. Please identify any unanticipated or otherwise unexpected immigrant groups who may come to South Florida.

12. What impacts would such groups have on the local government services identified in question 8?

Would you like this study's final report?
If yes, please complete:

       Name   _____
       Address   _____
       City, State, Zip _____
       Phone   _____

NATIONAL EXPERTS QUESTIONNAIRE

Please circle the percentage range appropriate for each country of origin.

1. What percentage of immigrants settling in Dade County will be undocumented?

Cuba	0-25%	26-50%	51-75%	76-100%
Haiti	0-25%	26-50%	51-75%	76-100%
Nicaragua	0-25%	26-50%	51-75%	76-100%
Guatemala	0-25%	26-50%	51-75%	76-100%
El Salvador	0-25%	26-50%	51-75%	76-100%
Honduras	0-25%	26-50%	51-75%	76-100%
Other:				
_____	0-25%	26-50%	51-75%	76-100%
_____	0-25%	26-50%	51-75%	76-100%

2. What percentage of immigrants settling in Dade County will be able to speak English?

Cuba	0-25%	26-50%	51-75%	76-100%
Haiti	0-25%	26-50%	51-75%	76-100%
Nicaragua	0-25%	26-50%	51-75%	76-100%
Guatemala	0-25%	26-50%	51-75%	76-100%
El Salvador	0-25%	26-50%	51-75%	76-100%
Honduras	0-25%	26-50%	51-75%	76-100%
Other:				
_____	0-25%	26-50%	51-75%	76-100%
_____	0-25%	26-50%	51-75%	76-100%

3. What percentage of immigrants settling in Dade County will have relatives, friends, or established communities of support upon arrival?

Cuba	0-25%	26-50%	51-75%	76-100%
Haiti	0-25%	26-50%	51-75%	76-100%
Nicaragua	0-25%	26-50%	51-75%	76-100%
Guatemala	0-25%	26-50%	51-75%	76-100%
El Salvador	0-25%	26-50%	51-75%	76-100%
Honduras	0-25%	26-50%	51-75%	76-100%
Other:				
_____	0-25%	26-50%	51-75%	76-100%
_____	0-25%	26-50%	51-75%	76-100%

4. What percentage will have white collar skills?

Cuba	0-25%	26-50%	51-75%	76-100%
Haiti	0-25%	26-50%	51-75%	76-100%
Nicaragua	0-25%	26-50%	51-75%	76-100%
Guatemala	0-25%	26-50%	51-75%	76-100%
El Salvador	0-25%	26-50%	51-75%	76-100%

Honduras	0-25%	26-50%	51-75%	76-100%
Other:				
_____	0-25%	26-50%	51-75%	76-100%
_____	0-25%	26-50%	51-75%	76-100%

5. What percentage will have blue collar skills?

Cuba	0-25%	26-50%	51-75%	76-100%
Haiti	0-25%	26-50%	51-75%	76-100%
Nicaragua	0-25%	26-50%	51-75%	76-100%
Guatemala	0-25%	26-50%	51-75%	76-100%
El Salvador	0-25%	26-50%	51-75%	76-100%
Honduras	0-25%	26-50%	51-75%	76-100%
Other:				
_____	0-25%	26-50%	51-75%	76-100%
_____	0-25%	26-50%	51-75%	76-100%

6. What percentage will have no job skills applicable in the United States?

Cuba	0-25%	26-50%	51-75%	76-100%
Haiti	0-25%	26-50%	51-75%	76-100%
Nicaragua	0-25%	26-50%	51-75%	76-100%
Guatemala	0-25%	26-50%	51-75%	76-100%
El Salvador	0-25%	26-50%	51-75%	76-100%
Honduras	0-25%	26-50%	51-75%	76-100%
Other:				
_____	0-25%	26-50%	51-75%	76-100%
_____	0-25%	26-50%	51-75%	76-100%

7. What percentage of immigrants settling in Dade County, Florida are likely to engage in criminal activity?

Cuba	0-25%	26-50%	51-75%	76-100%
Haiti	0-25%	26-50%	51-75%	76-100%
Nicaragua	0-25%	26-50%	51-75%	76-100%
Guatemala	0-25%	26-50%	51-75%	76-100%
El Salvador	0-25%	26-50%	51-75%	76-100%
Honduras	0-25%	26-50%	51-75%	76-100%
Other:				
_____	0-25%	26-50%	51-75%	76-100%
_____	0-25%	26-50%	51-75%	76-100%

8. The following question requests a high, low and most likely estimate of the total number of documented and undocumented new immigrants establishing residence in Dade County over the next year and the next ten years by specific countries of origin. The estimates will be used to develop a consensus of range.

	1989			1990-2000		
	Low Estimate	Most Likely	High Estimate	Low Estimate	Most Likely	High Estimate
Cuba	____	____	____	____	____	____
Haiti	____	____	____	____	____	____
Nicaragua	____	____	____	____	____	____
Guatemala	____	____	____	____	____	____
El Salvador	____	____	____	____	____	____
Honduras	____	____	____	____	____	____
Other:						
_____	____	____	____	____	____	____
_____	____	____	____	____	____	____

An important aspect in forecasting is the development of policy pertaining to the flow of documented and undocumented immigrants. The following questions address possible policy issues.

9. Will refugee status be granted to immigrants currently not eligible for such status in the next year?

yes___ no___

If yes, which country or countries of origin will be affected?

10. Will refugee status be granted to immigrants currently not eligible for such status in the next ten years?

yes___ no___

If yes, which country or countries of origin will be affected?

11 Will a resettlement program be established for incoming immigrants in the next year?

yes___ no___

If yes, which country or countries of origin will be affected?

12 Will a resettlement program be established for incoming immigrants in the next ten years?

yes___ no___

If yes, which country or countries of origin will be affected?

13. Will extended voluntary departure status (EVD) be granted to any immigrant group in the next year?

yes___ no___

If yes, which country or countries of origin will be affected?

14. Will extended voluntary departure status (EVD) be granted to any immigrant group in the next ten years?

yes___ no____

If yes, which country or countries of origin will be affected?

15. Please discuss any additional policy change areas that you feel will be of major importance to immigrants.

Would you like this study's final report?
If yes, please complete:

Name   _____
Address   _____
City, State, Zip   _____
Phone   _____

Bibliography

Armstrong, J. 1985. *Long-Range Forecasting: From Crystal Ball to Computer.* 2nd ed. New York: Wiley.

Basch, Kenneth. 1983. "Federal Responsibilities for Resettling Refugees." *Journal of Urban & Contemporary Law* 24: 151–192.

Blau, Francine. 1984. "The Use of Transfer Payments by Immigrants." *Industrial and Labor Relations Review* 37(2): 222–239.

Bogen, Elizabeth. 1987. *Immigration in New York.* New York: Praeger.

Borjas, George J., and Stephen J. Trejo. 1991. "Immigrant Participation in the Welfare System." *Industrial and Labor Relations Review* 44(2): 195–211.

Briggs, Vernon M. 1984. *Immigration Policy and the American Labor Force.* Baltimore: Johns Hopkins University Press.

Card, David. 1990. "The Impact of the Mariel Boatlift on the Miami Labor Market." *Industrial and Labor Relations Review* 43: 245–257.

Chickering, A. 1848. *Immigration into the United States.* Boston: C. C. Little and J. Brown.

Chiswick, Barry R. 1988. *Illegal Aliens: Their Employment and Employers.* Kalamazoo, Mich.: W. E. Upjohn Institute for Employment Research.

Clark, Rebecca L. 1994. *The Costs of Providing Public Assistance and Education to Immigrants.* Washington, D.C.: Urban Institute Press.

Collins, Nancy. 1991. *Do Immigrants Place a Tax Burden on New Jersey Residents?* Unpublished senior thesis. Department of Economics, Princeton University.

Cooney, Rosemary S., and Maria A. Contreras. 1978. "Residence Patterns of Social Register Cubans: A Study of Miami, San Juan, and New York SMSAs." *Cuban Studies* 8(July): 33–50.

Dade County Public Schools. 1989. *Student Population Data.* Miami: Dade County Public Schools.

Ferree, Myra M. 1979. "Employment without Liberation: Cuban Women in the United States." *Social Science Quarterly* 60(June): 35–50.

Frankenhoff, Charles A. 1985. "Cuban, Haitian Refugees in Miami: Public Policy Needs for Growth from Welfare to Mainstream." *Migration Today* 13(March): 7–13.

General Accounting Office. 1994. *Illegal Aliens: Assessing Estimates of Financial Burden on California*. Washington, D.C.: U.S. Government Printing Office.

Glaab, Charles N. 1967. *A History of Urban America*. New York: Macmillan.

Greater Miami Chamber of Commerce. 1985. Department of Labor, Health and Human Services, Education, and Related Agencies Appropriations for 1986. *Report of the Committee on Immigration Policy*. Part 10, pp. 691–723.

Greenwood, Michael J. 1979. "The Economic Consequences of Immigration for the U.S.: A Survey of the Findings." In *Interagency Task Force on Immigration Policy, Staff Report Companion Papers*. Washington, D.C.: Department of Justice, Labor, and State.

Heer, David M. 1990. *Undocumented Mexicans in the United States*. Cambridge: Cambridge University Press.

Hill, Kenneth. 1985. "Illegal Aliens: An Assessment." In *Immigration Statistics: A Story of Neglect*, edited by Daniel B. Levine, Kenneth Hill, and Robert Warren. Washington, D.C.: National Academy Press, pp. 225–250.

Huddle, Donald L., Arthur F. Corwin, and Gordon J. MacDonald. 1985. *Illegal Immigration Job Displacement and Social Costs*. Alexandria, Va.: American Immigration Control Foundation.

Jenson, Leif. 1987. "Patterns of Immigration and Public Assistance Utilization, 1970–1980." *International Migration Review* 22: 50–83.

Jones, M. A. 1960. *American Immigration*. Chicago, Ill.: University of Chicago Press.

Joy, Wayne. 1990. "Immigration: Its Impact on Florida and South Florida." Remarks at the Conference on the Future of South Florida. Sponsored by the Florida International University, Institute of Governments.

Katz, Barbara J. 1982. "Latins' Homicide Rate Jumps 300% since '74." *Miami News*, February, p. 1.

Keely, Charles B. 1982. "Illegal Migration." *Scientific American* 246: 41–47.

Lawless, Robert. 1986. "Haitian Migrants and Haitian Americans: From Invisibility into the Spotlight." *Journal of Ethnic Studies* 14: 29–70.

Levine, Daniel B., Kenneth Hill, and Robert Warren, eds. 1985. *Immigration Statistics: A Story of Neglect*. Washington, D.C.: National Academy Press.

Levitan, Aida T. 1980. *Hispanics in Dade County: Their Characteristics and Needs*. Miami: Office of the County Manager, Latin Affairs.

Linestone, Harold, and Murray Turoff, eds. 1985. *The Delphi Method*. Reading, Mass.: Addison-Wesley.

Loveless, Stephen, Dolores Brosnan, Clifford McCue, Dorothy Norris-Tirrell, Raymond Surette, and Lidia Tuttle. 1990. *Forecasting the Impact of Immigration on the Provision of Municipal Services in Dade County*. Miami: School of Public Affairs and Services, Florida International University.

Luytjes, Jan B. 1982. *Economic Impact of Refugees in Dade County*. Miami: Bureau of Business Research, Florida International University.

Massey, Douglas. 1990. "The Social and Economic Origins of Immigration." *Annals of the American Academy of Political and Social Science* 487: 181–200.

McCoy, Clyde, and Diana H. Gonzalez. 1985. "Cuban Immigration and Immigrants in Florida and the United States: Implications for Immigration Policy." Gainesville: University of Florida, Bureau of Economic and Business Research Monograph No. 3.

McCue, Clifford P. 1993. "Local Government Revenue Diversification: A Portfolio Analysis and Evaluation." In *Handbook of Comparative Public Budgeting and Financial Management*, edited by T. D. Lynch and L. L. Martin. New York: Marcel Dekker.

Mentzer, J., and J. Cox. 1984. "Familiarity, Application, and Performance of Sales Forecasting Techniques." *Journal of Forecasting* 3: 27–36.

Metropolitan Dade County Planning Department, Research Division. 1981. *Cuban and Haitian Refugees: Miami Standard Metropolitan Statistical Area—1980.* Miami: Metropolitan Dade County Planning Department.

Metropolitan Dade County Planning Department, Research Division. 1986. *Population Projections: Dade County, Florida, 1985–2010.* Miami: Metropolitan Dade County Planning Department.

Metropolitan Dade County Planning Department, Research Division. 1987. *Seasonal–Transient Population: Dade County, Florida.* Miami: Metropolitan Dade County Planning Department.

Metropolitan Dade County Planning Department, Research Division. 1988. *Annual Population Report: Dade County, Florida.* Miami: Metropolitan Dade County Planning Department.

Mohl, Raymond A. 1982. "Race, Ethnicity, and Urban Politics in Miami Metropolitan Area." *Florida Environmental and Urban Issues* 9(April): 21–37.

Muller, Thomas, and Thomas Espenshade. 1985. *The Fourth Wave: California's Newest Immigrants.* Washington, D.C.: Urban Institute Press.

Muller, Thomas, Carol Soble, and Susan Dujack. 1980. *The Urban Household in the 1980s—A Demographic and Economic Perspective.* Washington, D.C.: Urban Institute Press.

North, David, and Marion Houston. 1976. *The Characteristics and Role of Illegal Aliens in the U.S. Labor Market: An Exploratory Study.* Washington, D.C.: Linton and Company.

Office of the Dade County Manager. 1985. *White Paper on Immigration.* Miami: Dade County.

Papademetriou, Demetrios G., and N. DiMarzio. 1986. *Undocumented Aliens in the New York Metropolitan Area: An Exploration into Their Society and Labor Market Incorporation.* New York: Center for Migration Studies of New York.

Passel, Jeffrey S. 1985. "Estimates of Undocumented Aliens in the 1980 Census for SMSAs." Memorandum for Roger Herriot, August 16.

Passel, Jeffrey S. 1986. "Undocumented Immigration." *Annals of the American Academy of Political and Social Science* 487: 181–200.

Passel, Jeffrey S., and Karen A. Woodrow. 1984. "Geographic Distribution of Undocumented Immigrants: Estimates of Undocumented Aliens Counted in the 1980 Census by State." *International Migration Review* 18: 642–671.

Passel, Jeffrey S., and Karen A. Woodrow. 1987. "Change in the Undocumented Alien Population in the United States." *International Migration Review* 21: 1034–1323.

Pereira, Sergio. 1985. *Testimony before the Subcommittee on Census and Population Hearings on Demographic Impact of Immigration on the United States*. Washington, D.C.: U.S. Government Printing Office.

Perez, Lisandro. 1985. "The Cuban Population of the U.S.: The Results of the 1980 U.S. Census of Population." *Cuban Studies* 15: 1–8.

Perez, Lisandro. 1986. "Cubans in the United States." In *Immigration and American Public Policy*, Vol. 487 of the *Annals of the American Academy of Political and Social Science*, edited by Rita J. Simon. Beverly Hills, Calif.: Sage Publications, pp. 126–137.

Pindyck, Robert S., and Daniel L. Rubinfeld. 1981. *Econometric Models and Economic Forecasts*. New York: McGraw-Hill.

Portes, Alejandro, and Robert L. Bach. 1985. *Latin Journey*. Berkeley: University of California Press.

Portes, Alejandro, and Alex Stepick. 1985. "Unwelcome Immigrants: The Labor Market Experiences of 1980 (Mariel) Cuban and Haitian Refugees in South Florida." *American Sociological Review* 50(August): 493–514.

Portes, Alejandro, Alex Stepick, and Cynthia Truelove. 1986. "Three Years Later: The Adaptation Process of 1980 (Mariel) Cuban and Haitian Refugees in South Florida." *Population Research and Policy Review* 5: 83–94.

Portes, Alejandro, J. Clark, and R. Manning. 1985. "After Mariel: A Survey of the Resettlement Experience of 1980 Cuban Refugees in Miami." *Cuban Studies* 15(2): 37–59.

Rothman, Eric S., and Thomas J. Espenshade. 1992. "Fiscal Impacts of Immigration to the United States." *Population Index* 58: 381–415.

Simon, Julian. 1981. *What Immigrants Take from and Give to the Public Coffers*. Washington, D.C.: U.S. Immigration Policy and the National Interest, Appendix D to Staff Report of the Select Commission on Immigration and Refugee Policy.

Simon, Julian. 1984. "Immigrants, Taxes, and Welfare in the United States." *Population and Development Review* 10: 55–70.

Simon, Julian. 1985. *How Do Immigrants Affect Us Economically?* Washington, D.C.: Center for Immigration Policy and Refugee Assistance.

Simon, Rita J. 1982. *The Soviet Jews' Adjustment to the United States: Report of a Study*. New York: Council of Jewish Federation.

Solis, Humberto. 1981. "Hispanics in Tampa: A Socio-Demographic Study." Tampa: Florida State Commission on Hispanic Affairs.

Stepick, Alex. 1992. *Miami Now! Immigration, Ethnicity, and Social Change*. Gainesville: University Press of Florida.

Taft, Philip B., Jr. 1982. "Policing the New Immigrant Ghettos." *Police Magazine* (July): 10–27.

Tienda, Marta, and Leif Jensen. 1986. "Immigration and Public Assistance Participation: Dispelling the Myth of Dependency." *Social Science Research* 15(4): 372–400.

U.S. Bureau of the Census. 1993. *The Foreign-Born Population in the United States, 1990*. Washington, D.C.: U.S. Government Printing Office.

U.S. House Subcommittee on Immigration, Refugees, and International Law. 1981. *U.S. Refugee Program*. 97th Cong., 1st Sess.

U.S. Immigration and Naturalization Service. 1987. *Statistical Yearbook of the Immigration and Naturalization Service, 1986.* Washington, D.C.: U.S. Government Printing Office.

U.S. Immigration and Naturalization Service. 1991. *An Immigrant Nation: United States Regulation of Immigration, 1798–1991.* Washington, D.C.: U.S. Department of Justice, Immigration and Naturalization Service.

U.S. Select Commission on Immigration and Refugee Policy. 1981. *U.S. Immigration Policy and the National Interest: Final Report and Recommendations of the Select Commission on Immigration and Refugee Policy* to the Congress and President of the United States. Issued March 1, 1981. Washington, D.C.: U.S. Government Printing Office.

U.S. Senate Committee on the Judiciary. 1983. *Cost of the Cuban Flotilla: Hearing on Immigration Emergency Legislation.* 98th Cong., 2nd Sess.

Wallace, Steven P. 1989. "The New Urban Latinos: Central Americans in a Mexican Immigrant Environment." *Urban Affairs Quarterly* 25: 239–264.

Warren, Robert, and Jeffrey S. Passel. 1987. "A Count of the Uncountable: Estimates of Undocumented Aliens Counted in the 1980 United States Census." *Demography* 24: 375–393.

Weintraub, Sidney, and Gilberto Cardenas. 1984. *The Use of Public Services by Undocumented Aliens in Texas.* Austin: University of Texas at Austin, LBJ School of Public Affairs, Policy Research Project Report 60.

Winsberg, Morton D. 1979. "Housing Segregation of a Predominately Middle Class Population: Residential Patterns Developed by the Cuban Immigration into Miami, 1950–1974." *American Journal of Economics and Sociology* 38(October): 403–418.

Woodrow, Karen A., Jeffrey S. Passel, and Robert Warren. 1987. "Preliminary Estimates of Undocumented Immigration to the United States, 1980–1986: Analysis of the June 1986 Current Population Survey." San Francisco: Proceedings of the Social Statistics Section of the American Statistical Association meeting.

Wright, Louis B. 1971. *The American Frontier.* New York: Capricorn Books.

Yarnold, Barbra M. 1990. *Refugees without Refuge: Formation and Failed Implementation of U.S. Political Asylum Policy in the 1980's.* Lanham, Md.: University Press of America.

INTERVIEWS

Coordinator for Refugee Programs, Metropolitan Dade County.
Deputy Director, Immigration and Naturalization Service, District Seven.
Director, Office of Refugee Resettlement, Miami.
Director, Research Division, Metropolitan Dade County Planning Department.
District Director, Immigration and Naturalization Service, District Seven.

Index

ABOUT THE AUTHORS

The late **STEPHEN C. LOVELESS** was associate professor of public administration at Florida International University.

CLIFFORD P. McCUE is assistant professor of public administration at Kent State University.

RAYMOND B. SURETTE is professor of criminal justice and legal studies at the University of Central Florida.

DOROTHY NORRIS-TIRRELL is assistant professor of political science at the University of Memphis.

ISBN 0-275-94500-6

HARDCOVER BAR CODE